PROGRESSIVE

REVELATION

Hebrews 1:1-2…" God, who at various times and in various ways spoke in time past to the fathers by the prophets, has in these last days spoken to us by His Son, whom He has appointed heir of all things, through whom also He made the worlds"

John 14:26…" But the Helper, the Holy Spirit, whom the Father will send in My name, He will teach you all things, and bring to your remembrance all things that I said to you."

Romans 8:15-16…" For you did not receive the spirit of slavery to fall back into fear, but you have received the Spirit of adoption as sons, by whom we cry, "Abba! Father!" The Spirit Himself bears witness with our spirit that we are children of God, and if children, then heirs—heirs of God and fellow heirs with, Christ, provided we suffer with Him in order that we may also be glorified with Him."

2 Corinthians 5:20…" Therefore, we are ambassadors for Christ, God making His appeal through us."

INTRODUCTION

The common state of our understanding is either dull or dead. We are basically human. We accumulate knowledge for our own selfish purposes and then either abuse it, misuse it, or apply it out of context because of our limited view of situations and circumstances presented by the world around us. For the most part we function as orphans within a society of orphans striving for security and significance by any means necessary. We are dominated by our emotions and find no difficulty justifying our decisions through reason based on assumptions devoid of God's absolute Truth. The wisdom of man is accumulated from observance of the things in the world and even when 'new birth' is realized it is still difficult for immature Christians to accept the fact that they **can hear from God**.

In the first part of this book I will discuss the reality of the spiritual man who exists in both eternity and time simultaneously. Our failure to realize who we are "in Christ" after conversion leaves us ineffective as ambassadors of Christ and as conduits for the manifestation of His presence. If we have no concept of the Kingdom of God, we cannot effectively represent that culture in a world plagued by blindness. The wisdom of God that comes only through the Word of God by the Spirit of God is available only through the sons of God and it is only the mature sons who receive it. "Yet among the mature we do impart wisdom, although it is not a wisdom of this age or of the rulers of this age, who are doomed to pass away. But we impart a secret and hidden wisdom of God, which God decreed before the ages for our glory. None of the rulers of this age understood this, for if they had, they would not have crucified the Lord of glory. But it is written, *'Eye has not seen, nor ear heard, nor have entered into the heart of man the things which God has prepared for those who love Him.'* (1 Co.2:6-9)

Because the majority of the body of Christ is satisfied with remaining carnal, many use verse 9 as an excuse for their failure to 'grow up' in the grace God has provided. Our spiritual growth and maturity is in direct proportion to the revelation of the Kingdom we are open to receive for the purpose of fulfilling our God-given destiny.... sonship. God speaks to us via His Spirit before He speaks through us. The things we need to know for the life of Christ to be manifested through us are freely available to us on our journey to become the exact representation of our Father. **"But God has revealed them to us through His Spirit. For the Spirit searches all things, yes, the deep things of God." (1 Co.2:10)**

As a son of God who has moved from membership to discipleship to sonship, I am committed to the truth about who God says I am 'in Christ.' The second part of this book is a compilation of meditations that the Holy Spirit has shared with me progressively and that I have shared with others via weekly emails. I believe they are proof of how He speaks to us and works through us as we make ourselves available to His power and presence.

WHERE DID WE GO WRONG?

We have grown up with an understanding of the Bible that is full of holes that have not been filled. As religious converts we have accepted the notion that these holes will be filled when we get to heaven and until then we must accept what we do not understand from a God who will punish us is we do not obey. If you are still satisfied with that conclusion you have no concept of who our Sovereign Father really is and without this clarity you cannot possibly know who you are in His eyes. This is not uncommon when you consider the fact that most of our understanding of God and scripture is primarily intellectual and emotional and void of the guidance, direction, and the manifold presence of the Holy Spirit. Even our presentation of The Truth is basically derived from our continual eating from the tree of the knowledge of good and evil. It is highly unlikely

5

that everything we have been taught since we first learned is from Christ. There is much to learn, unlearn, and relearn and we must not be satisfied with being stuck on stupid by resting in our ideas about The Lord rather than being rooted and grounded "in Him."

We are trained to process everything mentally. That alone makes communication of any kind a virtual impossibility because all men were born in sin and therefore are mentally dysfunctional. We strive to understand things from a mental perspective and let our messed-up head speak to our heart instead of waiting for the direction of the Spirit. In our world seeing is believing while in the kingdom of Heaven the opposite is true. We live our lives based on what we know about in our head and not by what we KNOW in our hearts. The manipulation that results begins with our failure in knowing who we are. That knowledge is impossible for one who does not KNOW God for himself.

The book of Genesis informs us of the story of creation and says that God is responsible for ALL things created. Now, if you accept the truth of His Word you should also wonder **why** creation was necessary. The easiest explanation is that God and Love are one in the same. There is no true love without God because it is defined by His nature.

However, love cannot be defined except by demonstration. Just like faith and hope, love must be demonstrated to be seen. A Sovereign God decided to reveal Himself by creating a son through whom He could manifest His nature. But the key to understanding Genesis must begin with an understanding of the difference between eternity and time.

We live in and are familiar with the concept of time but are limited in our understanding of eternity. Even though we may have a desire to spend eternity with God, religion does not give us a complete explanation of what that means. Our view of life is limited to a linear perspective that keeps us in the dark about our future. It also leaves us with the responsibility of planning our own individual survival and manipulating others to secure our provision. This life of selfish ambition and existence began with the original sin and the tree of the knowledge of good and evil. The 'oneness' that God intended and requires is non-existent in the world and seldom seen in those who call themselves the children of God. God created everything, including mankind, and He does nothing without a purpose. His purpose for man was, and still is, sonship. God created a world and an environment that would be a reflection of heaven and His character and nature would be revealed through His sons. The relationship between

7

The Father and His sons would result in His sons becoming the exact representation of the Father because they would do only what they saw Him doing and say only what they heard Him saying. The kingdom of God would be extended from heaven to the earth.

God was not surprised by the rebellion of mankind that brought sin into the world and separation from The Source of all life. In fact, the salvation of mankind was provided for in eternity before the world, and man, was created. According to Revelation 13:8 "All who dwell on the earth will worship him, whose names have not been written in the Book of Life of **the Lamb slain from the foundation of the world**." THE LAMB was slain before the foundation of the world. The sacrifice for the salvation of mankind was made in **eternity** and then again **in time** at Calvary. The pre-creation covenant was a promise that God made to Himself that He would have sons. This covenant is the promise that those who, by faith, choose to accept the truth of the gospel of the kingdom will be delivered from the kingdom of darkness and translated into the kingdom of light and the family of God. They will be new creations...sons of God and ambassadors of Christ. By the power of the Holy Spirit they are authorized and empowered to fulfill the great commission as they are transformed into the likeness of Christ. They are the spiritual sons of God and blessed with new life that exist in both eternity and time simultaneously. They are a royal priesthood and a holy nation and vessels for His use to fulfill His plan and purpose in the earth.

"In our day again, the gospel of the kingdom has been replaced by an inadequate and false gospel, a gospel of personal peace and well-being. This false gospel loads believers with false assurances about their eternal state, even as it distracts them from the pursuit of holiness, minimizes the life of discipline and obedience, fosters and idolatry of material success, redefines the "go/tell" mission of the church, and leaves the larger issues of culture and society in the hands of the children of the kingdom of darkness.

The gospel of the kingdom has become captive to mere personal interest, felt needs, aspirations of prosperity, postmodern relativism, and social and political ambitions. Certainly, there are aspects of most of these in the gospel of the kingdom: however, the gospel of the kingdom is much broader, much deeper, much more integrated, and much more sweeping in its implications and power than any or all its present-day substitutes. "(Vishal Mangalwadi – Truth and Transformation)

ORIGINAL INTENT

You are 'born again' to GROW UP. The perpetual dysfunction evident in the lives of natural men is not intended to persist once one accepts the Truth of the Word of God and is endued with the presence and power of the Holy Spirit. Being born again is not about escaping to heaven when you die. Every living soul was born with a divine purpose and to discover that purpose one must grow to maturity. That knowledge and maturity also comes with the power and authority of the Kingdom of God. *"The Kingdom of God comes not with observation: Neither shall they say, Lo here! Or, lo there! for, behold, the Kingdom of God is within you." (Lk.17:20-21)* That power works in and through you to enable the very reason for which you were put here on the earth and it is your destiny. As a son of God your destiny is to become an exact representation of your Father.

A son of God is not a reference to male or female because God is not the Father of our flesh but of our spirits. *"There is neither Jew nor Greek, there is neither bond nor free, there is neither male nor female: for ye are all one in Christ Jesus." (Gal. 3:28-29)* Sonship is not a reference to your biological framework but to your spiritual descent out of the person of God. As a son of God, you may accurately conclude that everything that is said about Jesus is said about you. You were pre-destined to be conformed to the likeness of Christ...to that measure and standard. One of the greatest challenges is that as sons, God would not have us regard anyone according to the flesh. *"Therefore, from now on, we regard no one according to the flesh. Even though we have known Christ according to the flesh, yet now we know Him thus no longer." (2 Cor. 5:16)* As new creations our spirits have been assembled into the Body of Christ. *"The body is a unit, though it is made up of many parts; and though all its parts are many, they form one body. So it is with Christ. For we were all baptized by one Spirit into one body— whether Jews or Greeks, slave or free—and we were all given the one Spirit to drink. Now the body is not made up of one part but of many."*(1 Co.12:12-14). The 'new birth' makes us sons but we all arrive in a state of infancy. Our failure to grow up into mature sons keeps us carnal, unproductive, and ineffective in the fulfillment of our individual destinies and the great commission. Most Christians are still on milk and are satisfied with the bottle. We remain in Sunday school when it comes to our hunger for and understanding of the Truth. This results in the consistent drama that we either initiate, participate in or are entertained by as we engage in the survival we call life.

LET THERE BE LIGHT

Why did God create the heavens and the earth? *"In the beginning God created the heavens and the earth. **The earth was without form, and void**; and darkness was on the face of **the deep**. And the **Spirit of God** was hovering over the face of **the waters**. Then God said, **'Let there be light'**; and there was light. And God saw the light, that it was good; and God divided the light from the darkness. God called the light Day, and the darkness He called Night. So the evening and the morning were the first day. Then God said, 'Let there be a **firmament** in the midst of the waters, and let it divide the waters from the waters.' Thus, God made the firmament, and divided the waters which were under the firmament from the waters which were above the firmament; and it was so. And God called the firmament Heaven. So, the evening and the morning were the second day. Then God said, 'Let the waters under the heavens be gathered together into one place, and let the dry land appear'; and it was so. And God called the dry land Earth, and the gathering together of the waters He called Seas. And God saw that it was good. Then God said, 'Let the earth bring forth grass, the herb that yields seed, and the fruit tree that yields fruit according to its kind, **whose seed is in itself, on the earth'**; and it was so. And the earth brought forth grass, the herb that yields seed according to its kind,* *and the tree that yields fruit, whose seed is in itself according to its kind. And God saw that it was good. So the evening and the morning were the third day."* *(Gen.1:1-13)* The heavens and the earth were created to accommodate the purposes in the mind of God**. Both the heavens and the earth are created realms and are therefore not eternal.**

If you are like me your understanding of this passage has resulted in a complete misunderstanding of the creation story. We have read this multiple times without seeing what is said. Where was the earth "in the beginning?" The bible says that the earth was submerged in **the waters** and was **without form and void**. That means that the earth was not a ball in the firmament. It was not a thing that was formed and on the first day it was void of purpose. Since there was no space or clouds or precipitation there could be no H20, so what then is meant by the waters? The earth was submerged in the waters. **The Spirit** of God was hovering over the waters. Creation is a mystery without an understanding of **The Deep, The Waters, and The Spirit**. None of these existed in creation because creation did not yet exist.

The story of the woman at the well (Jn. 4:1-26) reveals the meaning of the waters**. "Jesus answered and said to her, "If you knew the gift of God, and who it is who says to you, 'Give me a drink,' you** *would have asked Him, and He would have given you living water." (Jn.4:10)* In creation, the water takes on the form of the Word. The deep represents God and contained within the deep is the water (Word) over which the Holy Spirit hovers. There is this inseparable connection between the water and the Spirit and the administration that is hidden in the water is by the Spirit. It is not possible to access the Word without the Spirit. The deep fills everything in every way and everything that is coming now, as it relates to creation, is hidden in the Word previous to creation. The Word is the Word because it is spoken to release what is in the deep. *Before creation the corporate nature of God...God Himself... existed as the deep, the Word, and the Spirit. That configuration of a corporate Father is manifested in creation as The Father, Son, and Holy Spirit*.

"This is the message which we have heard from Him and declare to you, that **God is light and in Him is no darkness at all.** *If we say that we have fellowship with Him, and walk in darkness, we lie and do not practice the truth.* **But if we walk in the light as He is in the light, we have fellowship with one another, and the blood of Jesus Christ His Son cleanses us from all sin.***"*   *(1 Jn.1:5-7) The* first five verses of Genesis introduce us to the concept of personhood without form. God is a Spirit who contains the Word which is Spirit and brings life. God decides to reveal

Himself by proclaiming "Let there be light." That light is who He is and represents His revealed presence in both eternity and time. He calls the light day. Ignorance of His presence is called darkness or night. Day one of creation speaks of a separation of light from darkness that is represented by day and night. The darkness is not eliminated but remains as a choice for mankind in creation and is called sin. Every living soul has to make the choice between living in the light or remaining in darkness. This choice was represented by the two trees in the garden. We are constantly tempted by the tree of the knowledge of good and evil in which there is no light or life. That tree is easily accessible through the will of man and results in man thinking he is a god apart from God. The tree of life is only accessible through the Spirit which brings light and life. Paul says of those who choose the truth of the gospel, *"You are all sons of light and sons of the day. We are not of the night nor of darkness." (1 Thes.5:5)* The purpose of creation is to host the presence of God both in heaven and in earth and the sons of God are challenged to walk in the light as He is in the light.

The first days of creation are about separation. **On day one** God said, "Let there be light." God separates the realms into light and darkness to demonstrate the choice that will lay before us in creation. Man is free to choose between darkness (death) and light (the revealed presence of God) …life in the daylight or a life in the darkness. When you walk in the light it is because you retain a conscious awareness of God. The whole world is in darkness and when you choose to live in that state you reject the plan and purpose of God for your life. This is called sin.

Creation was designed to host the manifested presence of God both in heaven and in earth. Our commitment to the truth is tested by trials. *"Beloved, do not think it strange concerning the fiery trial which is to try you, as though some strange thing happened to you; but rejoice to the extent that you partake of Christ's sufferings, that when His glory is revealed, you may also be glad with exceeding joy."* (1 Peter 4:12-13) As we are transformed into the image of Christ these trials allow for the implementation of the revelation we receive for every situation and circumstance. Revelation then moves to incarnation as we choose to submit to the Christ in us. We become Christ to others.

On the second day God separated the waters from the waters. *"Then God said, 'Let there be a <u>firmament</u> in the midst of the waters, and let it divide the waters from the waters.' Thus, God made the firmament, and divided the waters which were under the firmament from the waters which were* *above the firmament; and it was so. And God called the firmament Heaven. So, the evening and the morning were the second day.* The water is the WORD and the Word is the Son. He is the firstborn and the ruler seated on the throne. It was God's intention that your spirit be assembled to His Spirit so that you would be seated with Him in the heavenly realms. There is a Word above the firmament that holds heaven together. That Word is the weightiest thing that there is in creation that came out of the deep and the heavens were constructed to hold the weight. Heaven was created on the second day and designed to contain the throne of God as a picture of the authority of God over all of creation. This is the authority by which you are to function on the earth (Mt.28:18). "In Christ" you are a royal priesthood in the order of Melchizedek. You were designed to display the Glory of God as you are transformed into the likeness of Christ

There is the Word that governs heaven and the Word that governs the earth. That is the meaning of the separation of the waters. There are things that God reveals to the earth that are known but there are also secrets that must be revealed from heaven to the earth in their time and season. This is progressive revelation that is available only to and through spiritual sons who receive the answer to the request

"Thy kingdom come, thy will be done." The Word in heaven came to the earth and is the exact representation of the Father. He is the model for how we were designed to function in the earth by the power of the Spirit. Jesus lived, died, and was raised again and when we accept what He did for us that we could not do for ourselves we are empowered to operate in the earth from the theater of heaven. We are spiritual beings in earthly bodies engaging the Word that is greater than both heaven and earth. His life becomes our life, as God intended, and when those who are still in darkness see us, they see Him. The sons of God exist in both eternity and time at the same time. The waters in the heavens as the Word come into the earth in the form of the economy of the Kingdom of Heaven and is called "GRACE."

*Then God said, 'Let the waters under the heavens be gathered together into one place, and let the dry land appear'; and it was so. And God called the dry land Earth, and the gathering together of the waters He called Seas. And God saw that it was good. Then God said, 'Let the earth bring forth grass, the herb that yields seed, and the fruit tree that yields fruit according to its kind, **whose seed is in itself, on the earth'**; and it was so. And the earth brought forth grass, the herb that yields seed according to its kind, and the tree that yields fruit, whose seed is in itself* *according to its kind. And God saw that it was good. So the evening and the morning were the third day."*

The late pastor Miles Monroe said that God's original intent was to rule the visible from the invisible through the invisible in the visible on the visible. When God said, "let there be light" His intent was to become visible through what He created and put in creation. On day three God demanded that dry land appear and the waters above the firmament were separated from the waters below. The earth, which was formless and in the Word (waters), was formed and dry land appeared by God's command. The waters below the firmament are designed to remind us of the waters above the firmament and the earth and everything in it is analogous of that which comes from the heavens via the Word. The concept of death and resurrection is introduced in v. 11. All seed must go through a process in order to release the life within the seed and resurrection is descriptive of the presence of God in the earth to transform that which is in darkness, to that which is of the light. The Spirit of God is a life-giving Spirit and if we live in Him as He is in us we will never die. The resurrected life is a reality for all who are in Christ. When the old nature is dead the new creation that we are progressively reveals His nature as we are transformed into mature spiritual sons of God. The invisible becomes visible through us.

On the fourth day of creation God made the sun and the moon and the stars. There could be no possible way to determine the length of the first three days if there was no sun or moon until the fourth day. The rest of creation was completed on days five and six and concluded when God said, *"Let Us make man in Our image, according to Our likeness; let them have dominion over the fish of the sea, over the birds of the air, and over the cattle, over all the earth and over every creeping thing that creeps on the earth." So God created man in His own image; in the image of God He created him; male and female He created them.*

Man is made in the image of God and is therefore a spirit. When the breath (DNA) of God was imparted into a dirt body the soul was created...a living being with the capacity to manifest the nature of God in the environment to which he was assigned.

WANTS vs NEEDS...

God created a perfect environment and then placed within that environment a son. Adam was given dominion over everything in the earth and as long as he maintained his perfect 'father/son' relationship with God there were no issues. His relationship and his worship were evidenced by his 'growing up' under the love and instruction of The Father. Adam had no concept of negative emotions, no worries about provision and protection, no perspective other than that of his Father. Because he only knew God he only knew good. Because he had everything he needed he had no wants. Eve was not God's answer to a need but His revelation of the trinity of both God and man represented by the family. Marriage was God's idea and the husband, wife and child are representative of the Father (husband), Son (child), and the Holy Spirit (wife). Any other configuration of marriage is a deviation from God's plan.

Spiritual death is a disconnection with the source of all life. The original sin of Adam and Eve left mankind as orphans because of their unawareness of who their Father is. Adam did not suffer physical death for almost one thousand years because he was allowed to establish a culture that was the result of what he had learned from God. The original culture of the earth was reflective of the culture of heaven. The major flaw in the fall was that Adam lost the true perception of himself as a spirit and began to function from the perspective provided by his soul.

Man is a spirit created in the image of his creator. All of creation was designed to function and thrive according to the standard set by The Father. As a triune being man was designed by God to receive from Him. The body of man came from the earth and is therefore in tune with earthly things. The spirit of man was designed to accommodate direct communication with the Spirit of The Father. God speaks to man Spirit to spirit. This is not the case for one who has not been 'born again' because that individual is still in darkness and spiritually dead. The soul of man is that part of the trinity that needs to be saved. Without the benefit of direct communication with The Father, man is lost. He is not led by the Spirit but by his soul and like Adam he has lost his identity, purpose, inheritance, and his destiny.

MANIPULATION

The major components of the soul are the mind, the will, and the emotions. It is not difficult to see the resulting confusion in a world that is dominated by uncontrolled and unrestrained individuals who all have their own opinion, philosophies, and truths. Without the guidance of The Father we all make up our own minds about what reality is or should be. The strength of the will is always employed in the pursuit of our vision of reality. The mind determines what is real. Natural communication becomes difficult, if not impossible, because our individual goal is to convince the other person that our concept of reality is real. So what is normal in the natural world we live in is a community of dysfunctional orphans who have no awareness of who they are or why they are here engaged in either convincing or correcting each other of what they believe is the truth. This is not communication but manipulation.

When you consider the world we live in manipulation is the order of the day. Without the benefit of the awareness of a divine standard we are all victims of a universal marketing scheme that is designed to control our lives and make us predictable. All marketing is manipulation and our lives were programed by the rich and powerful before we took our first breath. This is because our parents were manipulated by the world as to how to raise us. Any advice that is not rooted and grounded in the Truth of God's Word is not aligned with the divine standard of The Father and is a form of manipulation. The world system which initiates and perpetuates the schemes of the devil is so subtle that we not only voluntarily submit to them but we pass them on to the next generation. The purpose of television is to manipulate through entertainment. An educational system that excludes the Word of God is controlled by an entity other than God and is therefore designed to manipulate. We will contest the distribution of opioids because of the danger to human life but we have no problem with putting a smart phone into the hands of every living soul,

23

including our children, that is one hundred times more addictive. If you think I am a little extreme answer this question. Do you prefer 'face book' or the bible? Sadly, most of the people you know have not made their relationship with God THE PRIORITY of their lives. The manipulation afforded by the world marketing system has convinced them that they do not need Him because if they stumble and fall they can pick themselves up and 'be great again.'

SEEK FIRST THE KINGDOM

This manipulation called marketing is not limited to the world. Religion is also a part of the problem. Instead of Christians living their lives as spiritual beings who know who they are and why they are here they have become primarily consumers. The genuine transformation of the sons of God will be reflected in the culture. Most churches have bought into the same lies that have replaced the culture of the kingdom of God with the traditions of men. We have become so ingrained in our religious traditions that we refuse to accept any truth that demands change and growth. This is true even when we continue to have questions that law and religion cannot answer. The information we receive, even in our churches, is often without a foundation that strengthens our faith and trust in Almighty God but in the institutional church. As long as we are operating only in the realm of time we will not be able to receive or understand the mysteries of God because they originate in the eternal realm and migrate into the earth by the revelation of the Holy Spirit to and through the mature sons of God. Our Sunday School mentality keeps us ignorant of the progressive revelation necessary to facilitate the spiritual growth needed to produce change agents in a world that rejects the light for darkness.

There is no relationship between the amount of information we accumulate and the ability to live a spiritual life. It is possible to become a theologian without having a personal relationship with The Father through Christ. Knowing about Christ and KNOWING Him are two different things. There is a direct correlation between the amount of information we gain and our level of frustration. Because we all have needs we often struggle with our own personal quest for satisfaction. Our physical health is a primary need that trumps all other needs when there is a physical problem. Once we are fairly certain that we are physically healthy we become aware of the need for personal worth. Our soul is convinced that in order for us to feel secure and significant we must complete our 'bucket list.' We hunger and thirst for those things that we have determined will make us worthy in our own eyes and the eyes of others. The resulting self-centered behavior is promoted by the pursuit of our false goals that can only bring a temporary satisfaction that leaves us right back where we began. This deficit motivation is met with frustration when we are trying to attain or produce something we are incapable of producing. This frustration is part of God's plan to help us avoid the feelings of self-pity, resentment, and anxiety that are unavoidable when we fail to recognize that personal worth can only be found "in Christ." The walking dead will never be satisfied. It is only when we become aware of our spiritual need (to love) that we able to manifest the Christ-centered behavior fostered by the biblical assumption "I am worthy because of my union with Christ."

THE TRUTH WILL MAKE YOU FREE

"You shall KNOW the Truth and the Truth shall make you free." (Jn.8:32) It is not possible to have an experiential understanding of eternal realities except through the divine revelation that comes by way of the Holy Spirit. Because we are raised in the temporal realm it is difficult for us to see and understand the eternal because we have to unlearn and be broken away from the temporal before the eternal becomes real. We approach the eternal from

a fleshly perspective and ask flesh questions. We assume that we can grow through more activity and dedication and commitment. We focus on more bible study, more church, etc. and are frustrated when those things do not bring life to our situation. The Spirit teaches us by bringing us to the place where we begin asking spirit questions instead of flesh questions. The Holy Spirit answers quickly and His answer is always in the present tense. It is always NOW and all we have to do is release the past and catch up with the answer. The answer to the mystery is always the same...Christ in you, the hope of glory.

TRYING, in the flesh, will never bring peace. Failure is a part of the growth process. We would never know the true life of the Spirit if God allowed us to succeed in the flesh. Our failures at living the Christian life press us into KNOWING Him as our life. *"But the Helper, the Holy Spirit, whom the Father will send in My name, He will teach you all things and being to your remembrance all things that I said to you." (John 14:26)*

"But as it is written, 'Eye has not seen, nor ear heard, nor have entered into the heart of man the things which God has prepared for those who love Him.' But God has revealed them to us through His Spirit. For the Spirit searches all things, yes, the deep things of God. For what man knows the things

of a man except the spirit of the man which is in him? Even so no one knows the things of God except the Spirit of God. Now we have received not the spirit of the world, but the Spirit who is from God, that we might know the things that have been freely given to us by God." (2 Cor.2:9-12) As new creations "in Christ" we are united with Him and the Holy Spirit reveals to us the deep things of God via progressive revelation. These things are freely given and we do not have to try to figure them out. When your understanding comes from your own fleshly efforts it will always be something that is earned. To know about means we must earn it. To KNOW means that we understand that it is freely given. I am not saying that we do not have to study to show ourselves approved. However, the satisfaction of our hunger and thirst for the truth comes by the Spirit through divine revelation. Then the Spirit leads us into situations and opportunities where we get clarity through the application of the revelation we have received. KNOWING is NOT thinking or feeling because once you know, you and what you know are one. You are united with the thing you know.

"At that time Jesus answered and said, 'I thank you, Father, Lord of heaven and earth, that You have hidden these things from the wise and prudent and have revealed them to babes. Even so, Father, for so it seemed good in Your sight. All things have been

delivered to Me by My Father, and no one knows the Son except the Father. Nor does anyone know the Father except the Son, and the one to whom the Son wills to reveal Him. Come to Me, all you who labor and are heavy laden, and I will give you rest. Take My yoke upon you and learn from Me, for I am gentle and lowly in heart, and you will find rest for your souls. For My yoke is easy and My burden is light." (Matthew 11:25-30) Through the experiential teach of the Holy Spirit we become one with the Truth. Because you and what you know are one there is no anxiety. God is in control and He has a lesson plan based on our individual experiences, needs, and desires that is unique to each one of His sons. The function of the Holy Spirit is to reveal the Father and the Son within us. Through transformation we progressively manifest the life of the Father and the Son.

"We always live out of what we know. It is practically impossible to walk in what we do not know. We receive a revelation and then get the experience of the revelation. The Holy Spirit works it into us, making us one with it. He does that through the noise and chaos of the seen and temporal realm: the world around us, our body and soul. These press us back into the knowing, into who we really are, into 'it is not I who live, but Christ lives in me.' That is where the real life is...where the real knowing is. We are

meant to know Him so that He can express Himself through us and become a 'well of water spring up to eternal life." (Sam Soleyn)

PROGRESSIVE REVELATION

God still speaks to and through His creation. Those who are still in darkness and ignorant of the power and presence of Almighty God cannot receive direct revelation from God because of the separation cause by sin. At the same time the earth and everything it is visible proof of His existence. God speaks to and through His sons.

"Then they said to Him, 'What shall we do, that we may work the works of God? Jesus answered and said to them, this is the work of God, that you believe in Him whom He sent." (John 6:28-29) We are spiritual beings created by God in His image for His plan and purpose. We were not designed to function independent of His provision and protection. We were designed to reflect His glory via our obedience. The Holy Spirit speaks only to the 'New Man'... the inner man, born of God. As new creations "in Christ" we are transformed into His image and as mature sons we manifest the nature of our Father. He speaks to us through nature, others, and the Word. The Word of God is life. ***"It is the***

Spirit who gives life; the flesh profits nothing. The words that I speak to you are spirit, and they are life." (Jn.6:63)

His divine revelation is progressive because He will not give you more than you are prepared to receive. As we learn to live by the Spirit we learn to ignore the useless efforts of the flesh. The question is not "does God speak to man?" The question is, are we listening? God gave you two ears and one mouth. As part of a royal priesthood we must learn to listen twice and speak once. As effective ministers of the truth we must first listen to what the world is saying, then to what God is saying about what was said. Then when we must only respond by allowing Him to use our mouth to say what He wants to say. God's Word is full of grace and truth and infinitely better than anyone's opinion.

"All praise to God, the Father of our Lord Jesus Christ, who has blessed us with EVERY spiritual blessing in the heavenly realms because we are united with Christ. Even before He made the world, God loved us and chose us in Christ to be holy and without fault in His eyes. God decided in advance to adopt us into His own family by bringing us to Himself through Jesus Christ. This is what He wanted to do, and it gave Him great pleasure. So we praise God for the glorious grace He has poured out on us who belong to His dear Son." (Eph. 1:3-6)   LIFE begins at new birth. This means you have no past that Satan can use to intimidate you and send you on a guilt trip. Your future is secure and you present life is lived in the 'NOW'. Every word, action, and reaction is directed by the power and presence of God. Your reality is that you are a heavenly being operating in time and that reality cannot be separated into components. You are a member of the body of Christ, the family of God. You are a part of a royal priesthood and a holy nation. You are a son of God and your body is not who you are but where you are. ***"All of you are Christ's body and each of you is a part of it."*** (1 Co.12:27) Our mission, as sons of God, is to deliver the message of truth in the character of Christ. As we are instructed and empowered by the Holy Spirit we are to "be Christ to others."

As I continue my journey towards becoming an exact representation of my Father I become more aware of the need to trust Him in EVERYTHING. I do not always understand what He is doing or why but by faith I trust Him without question. He speaks to me daily as I remain in and reflect His light. The remainder of this book contains some quotes but mostly conversations that my Father has shared with me on a regular basis. I have shared them with other via email on a weekly basis and I hope they will speak to you.

GROW UP! (Jn.17)

"Finally, be strong in the Lord and in His mighty power. Put on the full armor of God so that you can take your stand against the devil's schemes. For our struggle is not against flesh and blood, but against the rulers, against the authorities, against the powers of this dark would and against the spiritual forces of evil in the heavenly realms." (Eph. 6:10-12)

As sons of God and ambassadors of Christ we are called out to be the presence of Christ in the earth. We are empowered and clothed by the Spirit of God to confront the enemy and rescue those who are bound by darkness. That is why our enemy is not flesh and blood but spiritual forces of evil in the heavenly realms. Our enemy is not one political party or another, one political candidate or another, and not one human being or another. We lose our focus and our way when we get screwed up by these debates. We rush into battle against humans, against homosexuals, against abortionists, etc. The struggle is not against humans or against what humans are thinking but against the demons that put these ideas into their human minds. In a spiritual struggle we cannot focus our efforts on humans who are willing or unwilling pawns of the enemy. Our struggle is against the enemy of God and man, and us, who are the people of God. The struggle is a spiritual struggle.

The underlying root of every sin is Satan's manipulation of humans to wage war against God.

When we fail to understand this truth we confuse those who look to the church for Truth, clarity, and guidance. People don't know what to do because they don't know what we are doing. The power that you have from Jesus Christ is meant to be sufficient for your warfare in rescuing people out of the domain of hell and bringing them into the kingdom of God. The world needs to see the kingdom of God and the light of God's Truth as we become Christ to others by the power of His Spirit. Be bold and courageous and let Him live through you.

My shortest sermon: Shut up! Give up! Grow up! Get up and go.

THE GREATEST DANGER TO THE CHURCH TODAY:

- Christianity without Christ
- Religion without the Holy Spirit
- The Gospel without repentance
- Salvation without regeneration

- Politics without God

THERE ARE NO STUPID QUESTIONS...

Stupid: not intelligent: having or showing a lack of ability to learn and understand things. : not sensible or logical. : not able to think normally because you are drunk,

After facilitating a discipleship class recently, I was approached by a young man who said he had a question. He also stated that he had decided not to ask his question during the class because he did not want to be accused of asking a stupid question. I told him that there are no stupid questions.

If there is an answer to a question and the answer is not a stupid answer, the question is then no longer considered stupid. All questions originate from a lack of knowledge of a subject or circumstance. If a question is asked by one who genuinely is seeking the truth of a matter that person benefits from the information received. The answer itself eliminates the assessed state of stupidity by making it unnecessary to ever ask that question again. When the answer to your 'stupid' question results in gain and growth it also reduces the perception of stupidity.

Here is a revelation. All conversations, thoughts, and questions that are addressed and presented outside of the context of biblical truth are useless and unproductive because they cannot result in life and have no eternal value. They can only perpetuate and satisfy the illusion facilitated by our choice to continue to partake of the tree of the knowledge of good and evil. The only Truth is the Word of God. Those who refuse to accept His truth and the solution to the issues of life verify that there are no stupid questions, only stupid people.

BORN AGAIN?

Just exactly what does that mean? According to Romans 6 it means that by faith my old nature was crucified and buried with Christ. According to 2 Co. 5:17 it means that I am a new creation with no past and a secure future. It means that the guilt trip is over and everything I ever did and ever was is no longer a factor in my living in the NOW. I have been forgiven and my sins have been forgotten by God. It means that I am now united with Christ, a part of the family of God, a child of the King, a son of God who possesses the same power that raised Jesus from the dead. It means that as I grow in His grace I have the capacity to manifest the character of Christ every day and though the process of transformation be

Christ to others. It means that the only culture that counts, for me, is the culture of the Kingdom of God which is in me and surrounds me. It means that as an ambassador of the Kingdom I no longer need to give my opinion because I represent the King of kings and He now speaks through me. It means that I am holy and complete and righteous in Christ and He now lives through me. Jesus lives through me. He is my life. Because of my faith in God I now have the faith of God and am free from fear and shame. I am an awesome spiritual being with a God-given purpose. I am in this world but not of this world and the world sees Jesus when they see me.

When the body of Christ begins to BELIEVE the truth about who they are and learn how to love each other "as He loved us'" the world will see the sons of God as we practice what we preach.

"For in Christ lives all the fullness of God in a human body. So you also are complete through your union with Christ, who is the head over every ruler and authority." (Col.2:9-10)

ALL LIVES MATTER

The problem with this world is that we view all of our issues from a worldly perspective. We judge each other based on our own perceived position and condition and worth is determined by who we are, what we have and even by the color of one's skin. FEAR is the dominate emotion and because our thought processes begin there we cannot trust anyone or anything.

The recent uproar from the population is justified but misguided in the methodology used to address the issue. As a black man I am concerned about the fact that I have to consider a regular traffic stop by a policeman a potential threat to my life. However, the real problem is not the police department but the condition of the individual heart. Racism is systemic in the world and cannot be addressed until we admit that it is the problem. Rioting and killing only perpetuates the problem and increases the hate. Those who are unqualified to represent the population in any capacity because of their mental and emotional dysfunction must be rooted out and dismissed. But, we should not be manipulated by the system to act and react with a worldly response to a spiritual issue.

As a black man I am also concerned that we are quick go to the streets in protest when anyone other than us kills one of us. During the past 30 years 324 thousand members of our race have been killed as a result of black on black crime. How can we ask for the respect of others when we show so little respect for ourselves? Blacks compose approximately 14% of the population but are responsible for between 49-52% of the annual abortions. 870 black babies are murdered daily via abortion. It is obvious by the video evidence that there are incidences of prejudice that end in the death of an individual at the hands of those who are charged with protecting us. What is not so obvious is the disrespect we have for each other. We are so entrapped and manipulated by the world that we have no desire to accept the Truth of God's Word and trust Him to direct us in how to live and love each other. Jesus is the answer to the issues of life and there is no other solution.

According to science and my bible there is only one race...the human race. All men were created in the image of God and have the capacity to be transformed into His likeness. As the sovereign creator of everything God has a plan and purpose for every living soul. Until we individually accept His Truth, plan and purpose for our lives we will continue to spread the dysfunction that dominates a world system devoid of love. "What the world needs now, is love sweet love" can be voiced in a more accurate way. WHAT THE WORLD NEEDS NOW IS JESUS. Until each of us believes God's Truth and accepts His plan for this planet we will never be able to love one another, as He loved us. ALL LIVES MATTER.

A HOLY NATION...

Even an orphan is a citizen of a nation. The last hope of man for the assurance of provision and protection is in the laws and administration of a nation. This arrangement is subject to the control of the strong and the powerful and is increasingly coming under the influence of the skillful and unscrupulous.

The earth is in desperate need of a model of order and peace in which the problems of mankind are subject to permanent resolution. The solution lies in a nation of people that reveals the mystery of God the Father and Jesus the Son by demonstrating the goodness of God.

- Jesus prayed to the Father that the believers would all be one in the model of His relationship to the Father.

- Christ intends to present His relationship to the Father through this corporate form to the world, which knows neither the Father nor the Son.

- Since every human being belongs to a nation, God designed an expression of the Body of Christ to function as a nation among the nations of humankind. The governance of this nation must be clear and distinct so that it is observable to the world, and the quality of life that results from this form of governance bears a direct relationship to the order of this nation.

- This holy nation is designed to show how people from all of the divisions within the human community may be reformatted into spiritual families, households, clans, tribes, and ultimately, a nation capable of receiving any person in any condition and developing them to the place of a mature son of God.

- The prophecies regarding the order of the Church at the end of the age never speak of an urgent escape in the face of growing opposition. Instead, they present a picture of a people whose lives are characterized by righteousness, peace, and joy in an age of depravity, lawlessness, and chaos

- God originally gave Adam dominion over the earth to introduce this way of heaven within the natural creation. Jesus came to recapture this mandate and to give it complete expression as the template upon which His corporate Body would function.
- Daniel 7:26-28

Sometimes we get too comfortable in our skin and forget that we are spiritual beings who live in a body and are called to a specific purpose for the glory of God. His plan is for us to become sons of God as we are progressively transformed into the image of Christ. How committed are you to the process? Let me challenge you with these questions.

Is your Heavenly Father pleased with the way you are living your life right NOW?
If not, why?
Do you care?
If so, what are you going to do about it?

If you are not WILLING to do anything about the thing you are complaining about, STOP COMPLAINING about it!

UNITY

"I am praying not only for these disciples but also for all who will ever believe in me through their message. I pray that they will all be one, just as you and I are one—as you are in me, Father, and I am in you. And may they be in us so that the world will believe you sent me." (John 17:20,21)

It is impossible to achieve **UNITY** in the church through human effort. God's children need to realize that oneness must come through the cross and the crucifying of the flesh. There is no effective method of attaining unity without the experience of Calvary. No problem in the church is solved by human manipulation and ingenuity. Religion will not bring about reconciliation. The flesh and the natural can only damage the church and must not be allowed. The contributions and ministries of men are required but there must be the imprint of death upon them. Usefulness accompanied by the mark of death is called resurrection. The Lord Himself is the resurrection and His desire is to have a resurrection church.

LIFE

Most of the population of this earth has chosen survival over life. Survival is what we are accustomed to. Survival is rooted in selfishness. Survival is all about getting what we want when we want it by any means necessary. Failure to acquire our own desires alters our attitudes. Survival becomes difficult when we are not happy by our own individual standards or by the psychological manipulation we have submitted to.

Life, however, has been misinterpreted and misunderstood. Life, as we have defined it, is succeeding at survival. According to my bible true life, eternal life, comes only from God, our Heavenly Father, via His Son. True, eternal life is the life of Christ manifested through the sons of God, via the power of the Holy Spirit, through an obedient response to God's Holy Word. True life looks like Christ, acts like Christ, and believes like Christ. Life is acquired by those trying to survive when they accept the Truth of the gospel and surrender to that Truth. There is only one eternal LIFE and it is the life of Christ given to and shared by all believers as we are transformed into His image and used by our Father to manifest His character in a dark world that will only see His light through His family...through you.

Be INTENTIONAL with the life that God has given you.
PRACTICE WHAT YOU PREACH.

ONE LIFE...

So, whether you eat or drink, or whatever you do, do all to the glory of God. (1 Cor. 10:31)

Most of the people I know that call themselves "Christians" are confused as it relates to their identity and their purpose. They believe their life is their own and now that they have declared themselves Christians God is obligated to bless them and the decisions they make. They now live two lives by separating the secular from the sacredl...the private from the public.

News flash! A child of God does not have a private life. There can be no separation between the secular and the sacred. As new creations in Christ we have no past and our future is secure. By the power of the Holy Spirit we are eternal beings who live in the NOW. Like Jesus, everything we do should be what we see our Father doing and everything we say should be what we hear our Father saying. Paul says that our eating and drinking and everything else should reflect our relationship with our Father and glorify Him. This is not possible until we realize that there is only one eternal life and that is the life of Jesus Christ. As we are transformed into His image the only life that should become progressively visible is His life in and through us. Imagine what an impact we would have on the world we live in if our every earthly encounter resulted in the visible representation of our Father in and through us. What would happen if we truly functioned as ambassadors of Christ, witnesses for the Kingdom of God, containers for the manifestation of the power and presence of Almighty God? How would the world around us be changed if we trusted our Heavenly Father for our provision and protection, restricted our conversations to encouraging and not complaining, and became Christ to others? How different would your life be if you considered every moment of your existence to be sacred because you have been crucified with Christ and you no longer live but He lives through you.

If you are born again your life IS NOT your own. HIS life is now your life and there is no separation. How's that working for you?

NEW LIFE

"For ALL have sinned and fallen short of the glory of God." (Rom.3:23)

SELF-IMPROVEMENT is not only a sin, it is an impossibility. God's solution to our sin problem is that we must die and then be recreated as new creations with a new heart, mind, and spirit. The power of the gospel is that through it we are informed of THE TRUTH and by faith in that Truth we are identified with Christ in His death and resurrection. There is no remodeling or renovation of the human being in any shape, form or fashion. We are born again as sons of God and then progressively transformed into the image of Christ. He is in the Father and we are in Him and He is in us. It is His life that is seen in us and not ours. There is nothing we can or need to do to "be better." There is only ONE eternal life and it is His. You cannot improve on that. How's that working for you?

Your perspective is limited by the criteria you employ.

Without Christ it is impossible to be unselfish in a selfish world.

Every human decision is a statement of the character of the person making it.

SPIRITUAL WARFARE….

"But evil men and impostors will grow worse and worse, deceiving and being deceived. But you must continue in the things which you have learned and been assured of, knowing from whom you have learned them" (2 Tim.3:12-14)

Satan is a deceiver and as a deceiver he will work and prevail in good times and bad. "Success" and "defeat" does not define a work as being of God or Satan. Calvary stands forever as the revelation of God's way in working out His redemption process. Satan knows his time is short so he works for time, but God works for eternity. Through death to life, defeat to victory, through suffering to joy, is God's way manifested.

Man is deceived:

- If he is a hearer and not a doer (James 1:22)
- When he thinks he is 'something' when he is nothing (Gal.6:3)
- When he thinks he is wise with the world's wisdom (1 Co. 3:18)
- When he looks religious but is exposed by his tongue (Jas. 1:26)
- When he thinks he will not reap what he sows (Gal.6:7)
- When he thinks his own righteousness will get him into the kingdom (1 Co.6:9)

- When he thinks that contact with sin will not affect his life (1 Co.15:33)

Knowledge of the truth is the primary defense against deception.

You say you love God. Love and service are inseparable. How's that working for you?

ENCOURAGEMENT

One of the things a good salesman learns is the importance of complimenting the buyer on noticeable things as part of the sales presentation. This facilitates a safe and comfortable environment. During your daily encounters with family, friends, co-workers, etc. how often do you compliment them or give them positive encouragement? How often do you criticize, complain, or notify them of their short comings? Which do you believe is more beneficial?

As a child of God and an ambassador for Christ you are not to seek a balanced life but one of alignment with the Spirit of God. We are called to "be Christ" to others. That is only possible when be become one with Him. When we say only what we hear the

Father saying and do only what we see the Father
doing others will hear from Him through us. SPEAK
THE TRUTH, IN LOVE.

ALONG FOR THE RIDE (Gary Field)

Imagine if you had a friend

Who was always there by your side

To comfort and to lift you up

Whenever you were tired

If you knew He was the Godly sort

Who could not stand to witness sin

Would it have made you think twice

Before you snuck that shot of gin?

If he was there as a witness

Every time that you had lied

Or got involved in conflict

Because of jealousy or pride.

Would it make you feel uncomfortable?

If He watched as you did your dirt

Or would you try to put aside
Those things you know caused Him hurt.

Would you try to fine time alone
So that you would not feel the shame
When you did those things that would have shown
That you still played the devil's game?

Well, think of this the next time
That you try to sin and hide
The Spirit and the living God
Is always there inside.

And when you sin you invite Him in
To go along for the ride
To witness all those things you do
For which He was crucified.

How do you think it makes Him feel
When He sees through your disguise
And His wounds are reopened
Stung by the tears which fill His eyes.

You lie only to yourself

And the truth cannot be denied

Every time you sin my friend

You grieve the Spirit inside.

THE MATTER OF SEEING...

"Blessed are the pure in heart: for they shall see God." (Mt. 5:8)

Spiritual discernment (seeing) is not governed by thought but by the heart and is based on our consecration and obedience, not our cleverness and comprehension. Just because you may have a degree does not guarantee that you can see. True sight is the result of a pure and single heart. It does not require an object as large as the earth to blot out the moonlight. An impure heart is the cause of spiritual blindness. Singleness of heart is the test of absolute surrender. Only a pure heart can see and consecration is the sole condition for seeing the truth. The slightest doubt can change one's perception. Absolute surrender alone guarantees the ability to see.

LIGHTS ON!

"Let your light so shine before men that they may see your good works, and glorify your Father who is in heaven." (Mt. 5:16)

As sons of God we are in this world to manifest the character of Christ for the purpose of preventing corruption on one hand and condemning sin on the other. His light shines through us and the light ought to be put on a stand for all to see. Light is not heard; it can only be seen. Do people see the same thing in you that they have heard of you? Can others see that light to which you have testified? You are not only to persuade men but also to display the fact before them that you as a Christian are different from them.

Are your "light" and your "good works" one and the same thing. The act of shining is actually the nature of God being manifested in your life; it is not you. If it were only good works, people would simply give glory to us. The shining before men is a recognition that we are sons of God and that we belong to Christ.

HOW LONG?

A quick reading of Ps. 13:1-4, Rev. 6:10, and Hab.1:2 will reveal a personal sense of distress that is "all about me." It seems to me that we often offer lip service to a God we do not trust. We complain and question what we do not understand and expect Dad to fulfill our every desire. For some reason we have been taught to expect everything to be perfect because we have decided to follow Jesus. Are you serious? Have you read the four accounts of His life? Have you read the 38th chapter of Job?

"For I know the plans I have for you, declares the Lord, plans for welfare and not for evil, to give you a future and a hope." (Jer. 29:11)

Our lack of patience is evidence of our immaturity. In the Kingdom we have to go through something to get to something. You can't just google the answer to avoid the process. I imagine that our Heavenly Father could ask us the same question. HOW LONG?

- How long will you seek personal pleasure and ignore My plan and purpose for your life?
- How long will you claim to be a Christian while living in unbelief?
- How long will you complain about your life while rejecting the life I have ordained for you?
- How long will you continue to choose self-improvement over the guidance and direction of the Holy Spirit?
- How long will you blame ME and everyone else for all your problems while refusing to accept My Truth, plan, and purpose for your life?
- How long will you prioritize YOUR wants over the knowledge that "in Christ" you have all that you need?
- How long will you allow the temptations of the world to keep you from the benefits of the Word?
- How long will you allow your religion to keep you from a true relationship with your Heavenly Father?
- How long will you continue to trust everything but God?
- How long will you live your life searching for love in all the wrong places and ignore the fact that God

loves you more than He loves
Himself?

**"For whoever would save his life will lose it,
but whoever loses his life for my sake will
find it." (Mt. 16:25)**

HOW LONG is not a question to be asked by a
son of God. It assumes that we are waiting on
Him when He is actually waiting on us to *"Shut
up, Give up, Grow up, Get up and Go."* We
have ALL we need "in Christ" to fulfill the destiny
He has ordained for each of His children.
............*GOT JESUS?*

BIPOLAR CHRISTIANS

Bipolar disorder, also known as manic-depressive
illness, is a brain disorder that causes unusual
shifts in mood, energy, activity levels, and the
ability to carry out day-to-day tasks.

There are four basic types of bipolar disorder; all of
them involve clear changes in mood, energy, and
activity levels. These moods range from periods of
extremely "up," elated, and energized behavior
(known as manic episodes) to very sad, "down," or
hopeless periods (known as depressive episodes).

Less severe manic periods are known as hypomanic episodes.

I would submit that bipolar disorder is a normal condition of the flesh and is only classified as a "disorder" when it becomes so serious that it interferes with the normal worldly insanity that we have become accustomed to. As members of the "Adams family" we were all born in sin and raised in blindness, confusion, and ignorance of God's truth. Under those conditions we spend our lives trying to be who we think we are or who others want us to be. This is the condition of all men before they are introduced to the gospel of Christ Jesus and the kingdom of God. True self-awareness is an impossibility for the sinner who does not know Christ.

Truth be told, most "Christians" were converted into a religion and have no real concept of what a relationship with The Father through Jesus is all about. They have a spiritual bipolar disorder caused by a misunderstanding of Romans 7 and a constant striving for completion of a rehabilitation program designed to reach a level of self-improvement that will be pleasing to God. They attempt to follow church doctrine through a strict adherence to a list of do's and don'ts and become "good" children of God. They do not believe that "in Christ" they are complete, unconditionally loved, righteous, forever forgiven, and holy. They either forget or don't believe that they are dead to sin and alive to God (Rom.6:11) and that now there is no condemnation for those who are in Christ Jesus (Rom.8:1).

Jesus made the life He ordained for us simple with His last command…"Love one another as I have loved you (Jn.13:34). Until we learn to accept His life and give up our own selfish nature we will never be able to "be Christ to others." True sons of God are not bipolar because we only have one nature…the nature of our Father via the power of the Holy Spirit.

WE ONLY QUESTION WHAT WE DO NOT BELIEVE. Our ACTIONS are the product of our beliefs. Our UNDERSTANDING is the fruit of obedience.

DANGEROUS is the man who has nothing to live for and accepts that belief as truth. Even more dangerous is the man who, because of the promises of God, has everything to live for and rejects that truth. BELIEVE.....RECEIVE.....LIVE!

WHAT ARE YOU WEARING?

I often get positive comments on the fragrance of my cologne. I have never been one to wear multiple fragrances. I have narrowed my choices to two brands and won't even try anything else. My belief is that if you are going to wear a fragrance it should be impressive enough to introduce you. By the time you open your mouth your cologne (or perfume) should have already provided at least 40% of the conversation you would have said before you said anything. It should be bold without being loud and at the same time humble. It should leave those around you waiting for the rest of your conversation and hoping you don't leave soon. I wear Izzy Miyake and Creed.

As a son of God and an ambassador of the kingdom it should be evident to those who recognize the truth when they see it that I am different from most....a peculiar person. The light of the gospel and the glory of God should be reflected in my actions and my character. My belief that as a new creation in Christ I am everything He says I am should be evidenced by my walk and not just my talk. My humility should be accentuated by a divine boldness. As I am transformed into the image of Christ I am becoming the exact representation of my eternal Heavenly Father right Now. I have put on Jesus.

What are you wearing?

PERFECTION begins with acknowledging God for who He is and then submitting to His plan and purpose for the life He has ordained for you. It is then that the transformation process begins and you are progressively enabled by the power of the Holy Spirit to manifest the character and nature of Christ. This is evidenced by the way you love your brother and a hunger and thirst for righteousness that cannot be satisfied via the flesh. Searching for the truth with your head (flesh) will only result in more questions and confusion. Accepting the Truth by faith and obedience to the Word will bring understanding. Feed you faith and not your flesh. STOP trying and START TRUSTING.

"But as it is written, Eye hath not seen, nor ear heard, neither have entered into the heart of man, the things which God hath prepared

for those who love Him. <u>BUT GOD HAS REVEALED THEM UNTO US BY HIS SPIRIT</u>*: for the Spirit searcheth all things, yea, the deep things of God."* (1 Co.2:9-10)

God reveals, to His children, EVERYTHING we need to know...not everything we want to know. If we trust and obey and believe that He cannot lie we eliminate the need for doubt and confusion. Do you believe Him? Do you trust Him? Will you obey Him? If your answer is yes, He can use you for His divine purpose. *Shut up! Give up! Grow up! Get up & Go!*

GOOD IDEAS

Drama is impossible to avoid in the world we live in. GOOD IDEAS are the reason for much of our drama and confusion. Because we choose to continue to eat from the tree of the knowledge of good and evil we offer our ideas to even those who have not asked for them. Our failure to submit to the Spirit led life allows us to 'play God' when we offer our suggestions to others as a 'better way' of doing or being. We want to help others and we think we are always right. The problem is that if our 'good idea' is not God's idea, it is the wrong idea.

"Trust in the Lord with all your heart, and lean not on your own understanding; in all your ways acknowledge Him, and He shall direct your paths." Prov.3:5-6

The next time you have a 'good idea' that is not supported by Scripture and the prompting of the Holy Spirit try to keep it to yourself. Everything that originates from the flesh can only promote more drama and confusion. It takes practice to allow God's love to dictate your conversation with others. He is the One they need to hear.

THE TRUE CHRISTIAN LIFE

20 I have been crucified with Christ and I no longer live, but Christ lives in me. The life I now live in the body, I live by faith in the Son of God, who loved me and gave himself for me. (Gal.2:20)

The daily life of the true Christian can be summed up in one word...'receive'. We are challenged by God to allow Him to manifest His character and nature through us. Long-suffering, meekness, humility, goodness, holiness and joy are not virtues I acquire or things that I attain but each is the manifestation of Christ Himself. Christ in me meets every demand of God, and every demand of the circumstances around me. It is not in me to be humble or trustworthy, or obedient in the natural. These are not virtues to which it is possible for the natural man to attain. Christ is all of these and by His very nature He is the life you see in me. My righteousness, redemption, holiness and sanctification are not virtues but Christ in me, the hope of glory. He is all I need.

TRANSFORMATION

In his new book, America at the Crossroads, George Barna accurately examines ten stops on the journey to becoming Christlike that are experienced by every Christian. He notes that during the first 3 steps people progress from being unaware of the concept of sin to feeling indifferent toward the concept, to showing concern about the personal implications of sin but without doing anything about it. His research indicates that two-thirds of all Americans never get beyond these three steps even when regularly attending Christian churches. He points out that those who acknowledge that they are sinners, accept God's forgiveness, and embrace Jesus as both Lord and Savior master stop four and move on to stop five of the journey. They become immersed in religious activity with the hope of becoming better people and hopefully Christlike. His research shows that about one-quarter of the nation's population gets to remain at one of these two steps.

At stop 6 about half of the converts drop out as a result of being overwhelmed with its requirements. This is the place of spiritual discontent. The real challenge is presented by the last 4 least pursued and highly rewarded stops. Stop 7 is where one has to choose between the world and the Word. It is where we experience brokenness of sin, self, and societal control. That is followed and evidenced by a life characterized by the love of God as the basis for all our actions and the fruit that follows. These individuals are highly unusual and peculiar people because of who they have become rather than what they have done or what they know. This is holistic spiritual transformation.

"Unfortunately, seminaries do not teach pastors to encourage and facilitate such transformation; elder boards do not evaluate pastors based on their ability to foster transformation; sermons rarely address the practical realities of transformation; our culture, supported by churches, successfully implores adults to reject or avoid brokenness; and people doggedly pursue success and comfort rather than holiness. Consequently, most church-going people are involved in religion rather than genuine discipleship." (Barna)

Alpha Ministries and Dominion Ministries are committed to help those who are serious about getting past stop 6 on the spiritual transformation journey. Call me or contact us at any of the web sites or email addresses below and lets grow together by the power of the Holy Spirit, "in Christ."

DRAMA

You cannot escape it. That's because it either surrounds you or originates from you. The external drama that we encounter is unavoidable. It's the way the world works. Because man is born dysfunctional and in sin, every individual believes he/she is right about everything. How can that be possible if we learn just about everything from other dysfunctional individuals? All of our inquiries originate from selfishness even when we have good intentions. Our actions and conversations are often misinterpreted by those who can only see things their way or respond based on their emotions.

The resulting external drama is what we call normal and life is about learning how to deal with predictable insanity.

There is also an internal drama that becomes apparent once we become aware of the Truth. As born again Christians we are new creations who have a new heart, mind, and a new Spirit. We are no longer the dysfunctional person we used to be but have a new identity "in Christ." We are dead to sin and alive to Christ and are blessed with the capacity to manifest the character and nature of our Heavenly Father. The internal drama we experience comes from forgetting who God says we are now and struggling with the old man who is dead and buried. Don't be alarmed. That is a sign of growth and proof that there has been a change. If we continue to believe the truth of God's Word and are led by His Spirit we will progressively experience the Sabbath rest He promised to all His children. The world's drama leads to death. The Word's drama brings life and peace.

"There is now no condemnation for those who belong to Christ Jesus. And because you belong to Him the power of the life-

giving Spirit has freed you from the power of sin that leads to death." (Rom.8:1,2)

FELLOWSHIP

Abraham moved to Hebron (Gen.13:18), and there built his third altar. Hebron means 'a league'. In New Testament terms we would substitute the word 'fellowship' for it is through fellowship that the shared life of Christ is put to the test. Bethel represents the life in the Body of Christ and Hebron represents the principle of living that life. We must go through Bethel to get to Hebron. You cannot take a group of men and put God's principles of fellowship into them. Fellowship in Christ is both natural and effortless because it stems from the fact of the living Body of Christ, and there is therefore no need to plan or organize it. It flows spontaneously when our hearts are as was Abraham's, 'unto the Lord'.

All media is employed for one of three purposes: revelation, information, or manipulation. In the selfish, dysfunctional world we live in only revelation can initiate positive change. All other information only serves as a means of manipulation.

THE GIFT OR THE GIVER?

"Isaac can stand for many things. He represents many gifts of God's grace. Before God gives them, our hands are empty. Afterwards they are full. Sometimes God reaches out His hand to take ours in fellowship. Then we need an empty hand to put into His. But when we have received His gifts and are nursing them to ourselves, our hands are full, and when God puts out His hand we have no empty hand for Him. We can dwell on His gifts at the neglect of Him. Often we forget that our experience is not for our life-long use. Our source of life is God, not our experience. We hold on to the experience and forget God is Father. Let go the gift and the experience, and hold on to God. Isaac can be done without, but God is eternal." (Watchman Nee)

CHOICES

Man, is the only creature made in the image of God. We are triune beings just like God is. We are three-in-one…body, soul, and spirit. For man to properly function as God intended that order must be reversed…spirit, soul, body. Man, has only one problem, SIN. When Adam sinned he, and all men born after him, became victims of the enemy and a part of the walking dead. Spiritual, and eventually physical death, would be the fate of every soul. It is what we all have in common as members of the Adams family.

Before God created man, He devised a plan and made provision for the salvation of mankind which would restore life to those who believed and accepted His 'way'. Once we become aware of the gospel of the kingdom we also are invited to be delivered from the kingdom of darkness by faith alone. Part of that gospel is the knowledge of what Jesus has done for us that we could not do for ourselves. God solved man's problem before He created man. Spiritual death resulted in a union of our soul and spirit. Choosing to believe and accept the Truth releases our spirit and joins us to Christ in a way that gives us a new identity as we are progressively transformed into the likeness of Christ. We are born in His image. We are transformed into His likeness. We are born dead. We can choose life. We have the choice of remaining in darkness or we can choose LIFE. What is your choice?

One cannot see God through the eyes of the world. When you look at the world through the eyes of God, you will see him.

RECONCILIATION

TRY SOMETHING NEW! When you criticize another person you effectively criticize what God has made. Our Heavenly Father does nothing without a purpose. Instead of complaining about a soul that is made in the image of God, why not pray for them. It is difficult to do both at the same time. **"From now on, therefore, we regard no one according to the flesh. Even though we once regarded Christ according to the flesh, we regard Him thus no longer" (2 Cor. 5:16)**

Just as Jesus demonstrated, as ambassadors of Christ ALL of our actions and reactions must be founded in love and focused on 'the other.' Again, all humans were created in the image of God but when it comes to His likeness there is much work to be done. To attain to His likeness requires both 'new birth' and transformation. It is only by the work of the Holy Spirit that one can fulfill his/her God-given destiny and be conformed to His likeness. The newborn child must be raised up by the Spirit and in the Word to maturity. **"Wherefore if any man is in Christ, he is a new creature: the old things are passed away; behold, they are become new." (1 Co.5:17)** Those of us who are aware of our new identity 'in Christ' are to allow Him to live in us in a manner that results in the manifestation of His character through us. The ministry of reconciliation that we are charged with is not fulfilled or enhanced by any act on our part that is not initiated by the Divine Love of Almighty God. **"All things are of God, who reconciled us to Himself through Christ, and gave unto us the ministry of reconciliation." (1 Co.5:18)**

As an ambassador of the Love of God let your words be His Word. Let your acts be His acts.

Let the comments you post on social media reflect His love to a world He died for. In your everyday activities as His son be about your Father's business and 'be Christ' to others. As He loves you, love one another.

SPIRITUAL MATURITY...

Spiritual maturity, or maturity of any kind, is not attainable without access to the revelation knowledge of Almighty God. The wisdom and discernment that comes via the presence of the Holy Spirit verifies maturity. It is the calling and purpose of the mature sons of God to manifest the character and nature of God in a world cursed with blindness.

Man was created in the image and likeness of God and given dominion over the earth and everything in it. Through his relationship with The Father the intent was for man to rule in such a way that the physical world would reflect the spiritual headquarters called heaven. Humans were created by God to function as His family and are not to conform to the natural but rule and reign in the Spirit. In a sinful, selfish, dysfunctional world God rules through His mature sons. HE STILL REIGNS.

WHO ARE YOU? WHAT IS YOUR PURPOSE? Where are you in the transformation process as it relates to total submission to His plan and purpose for your life as an ambassador of the love of God? Have you decided to "be about your Father's business" or are you still trying to take care of your own? When will you GIVE UP trying to run your life according to your own understanding? When will you SHUT UP and stop asking questions, making decisions, and giving advice out of personal blindness and ignorance? When will you GROW UP into maturity by learning to listen and hear His voice and trust in His Word for your security and significance? And if you have attained a level of maturity which qualifies you to step out on faith and 'be Christ' to others, when will you decide to leave the salt shaker and GET UP AND GO and make disciples.

Consider Gen.1:26-28; Romans 1:18-32. The politics of born again Christians is very simple.

We live under a theocracy. Our life is simplified because God is the sovereign ruler.

We often attempt to understand spiritual truths with the natural mind while ignoring our limited capacity to understand natural realities with the same tool. How can we present a gospel we do not understand? How can we understand without the guidance and direction of the Holy Spirit via the engagement of the mind of Christ?

Before God will use your voice, He will teach you how to keep quiet.

Before God will use your feet, He will teach you how to keep still.

Before God will use your hands, He will teach you how to feel His touch.

Before God will use your eyes, He will teach you how to see with His.

Before God will use your intellect, He will give you the mind of Christ.

Before God will use you for His plan and purpose, He will show you how to suffer.

LIFE is not the individual experiences of many who fail to distinguish the difference between survival and living. **LIFE** is the experience of **THE ONE** who is the source of all life, shared by many. Without Jesus, there is no true life…. only survival. There is only one life. Until my life and your life become His life, true life as God intended is an impossibility.

God is always ready to give us what we need. We are not always ready to receive it.

THE TRUTH ABOUT CHRISTMAS

This is not going to please most of you but the truth seldom does. Christmas was not God's idea. The celebration of the birth of Jesus on Dec. 25th was not initiated by the first century church and has its roots in Roman custom and religion. The first Christmas celebrations were in reaction to the Roman harvest festival Saturnalia which honored Saturn, the god of sowing. Emperor Constantine initiated the celebration around 336 A.D. and then Emperor Justinian made it a civic holiday in 529 A.D. This was not an act of God but the result of the works of men. In the Scriptures, no one is recorded to have kept a feast or held a great banquet on Jesus' birthday. The Christian explanation for the celebration was the worship of The Christ by focusing on giving, family togetherness, feasting, etc. For good measure many other customs were included such as a decorated tree, lights, music, yule logs, and even Santa Claus.

Since most retailers realize up to 60% of their profits during this 'holiday season,' it is highly unlikely that this holiday celebration will be eliminated. The world celebrates Christmas without Christ and since the worship of Christ originates with the Spirit, so do many Christians. Many consider this "season" as a time of giving and adopt an entirely new attitude for a few weeks to appease their guilt and feel better. We do everything we can to meet the demands of those we love and hardly notice that the world has its hand out everywhere we go.

CHRISTMAS IS NOT AN APPEAL BUT AN ANNOUNCEMENT. This 'season' affords us the perfect opportunity to witness to others the truth about the coming of the baby Jesus into the world and the reason for His coming. "**So we also, when we were children, were held in bondage under the rudiments of the world: but when the fullness of the time came, God SENT forth His Son, born of a woman born under the law, that He might redeem them that were under the law, that we might receive the adoption of sons." (Gal.4:3-5)**

The significance of the manger in Bethlehem can only be understood within the context of the complete story of God's plan and purpose for mankind....SONSHIP. RECONCILIATION is God's plan for mankind and the sons of God cannot restrict the celebration of the birth of Christ to one day a year. If we are to be ambassadors of Christ and a royal priesthood and a holy nation we must make this announcement...this declaration of what God has done for us that we could not do for ourselves... EVERYDAY. For the mature sons of God the celebration of the birth of Jesus is a daily reality that is evidenced by us loving each other the same way that He loves us. It is always preceded by new birth and not by 'black Friday."

I am not attempting to kill Christmas. I am saying that for true sons of God we are called to live our lives as a daily celebration of the truth about the birth of Christ. Imagine what message we would send to those around us if we ceased to conform to the world and lived our daily lives as if every day were Christmas. PRACTICE WHAT YOU PREACH!

GOT JESUS....does He have you?

SPIRITUAL RICHES IN CHRIST

"I thank my God always concerning you, for the grace of God which was given you in Christ Jesus; that in EVERYTHING you were enriched in Him, in all utterance and all knowledge." (1 Co.1:4-5)

Compared to child of God the natural man lives in poverty. He is:

- 'Poor' in time and if not regenerated, poor in eternity.

- 'Poor' in utterance due to lack of knowledge. His conversations have no eternal value.

- 'Poor' through possessing earthly wealth. "You can't take it with you."

- 'Poor' because he is without Christ, who strengthens all things.

Those who accept the truth of the Word of God are united with Christ and regenerated by the power of the Holy Spirit and enriched by grace. As sons of God our birthright is restored and our inheritance secured. We are:

- 'Rich' in utterance because we are enriched by the knowledge of who God is and who we are 'in Christ.'

- 'Rich' through the freedom of not being possessed by the world's wealth.

- 'Rich' in Christ, in whom dwells the fullness of the Godhead bodily.

In Christ we are enriched in ALL our relationships because we have EVERYTHING we need in Him.

TRUE FELLOWSHIP

We are always learning (hopefully). There is a fundamental lesson specific to each of us that we must learn to function as God intended. Once that happens nothing can be the same again. We are then allowed to enter a new experience of the life of the Body of Christ which draws us together with all who belong to Him. It is then that the fruit of the Holy Spirit begins to manifest itself. Until the flesh has been dealt with we do not value fellowship. Fellowship means, among other things, that we are ready to receive Christ from others.

BOREDOM..

Are you often bored? Don't worry because it's natural. Boredom is the result of living the natural life. It is the result of the absence of Christ as your life. Notice that I did not say in your life.

When we live in the natural as carnal Christians, we seek happiness from the world and its' systems. Our boredom can only be satisfied temporarily by the things we lust for and eventually those things become boring. There is no true Life without the presence and power of the Holy Spirit. Lies and false promises are all we can expect from the world. As new creations "in Christ" we are delivered from the kingdom of darkness into the kingdom of light. As we are transformed into His image the old dead man disappears and the life and nature of Christ is manifested through our mortal bodies. We become Christ to others and when that is what is happening consistently boredom is an impossibility.

If you are bored it is because you are still in charge. Newsflash…you never have been and never will be. Trust Him. Let Him live His life through you.

For God wanted them to know that the riches and glory of Christ are for you Gentiles, too. And this is the secret: Christ lives in you. This gives you assurance of sharing his glory. (Col.1:27)

GOT JESUS? Does He have you?

THE PROBLEM WITH SELFIES...

"And we, who with unveiled faces all reflect the Lord's glory, are being transformed into his likeness with ever-increasing glory, which comes from the Lord, who is the Spirit." (1 Co.3:18)

The work of the Holy Spirit is the work of transformation. Every living soul is made in the image of God and is therefore a trinity (spirit, soul, body). We are spiritual beings housed in a body of flesh and our souls (personalities) reflect our true nature. Those who are unsaved reflect the nature of the Adams family. Those who have accepted the Truth of God's Word are progressively being transformed into the 'likeness' of God as it relates to their nature.

Looking good has more to do with how you act than physical appearance. God's children should be aware that the selfie you take is also a witness of your condition and position. What is the reason for the picture? Does it glorify the flesh by displaying your pride in your personal appearance or does it glorify your Heavenly Father by displaying His nature through you? Unless you are looking more and more like Christ, your selfie is all about you.

GOD'S WORKMANSHIP

For we are God's handiwork, created in Christ Jesus to do good works, which God prepared in advance for us to do. (Ehp.2:10)

"The sons of God never have to strive in order to please the Father; nor are they on an adventure of trying to learn how to communicate with Him. They function from the basis of knowing that they are in Christ and that He is in them. Their relationship with Him is from a place of oneness. Prophetic beings subject themselves to the likeness and nature of the one they come from— God. All of His characteristics and attributes are in us. Because He is love, we are love; He is joy making us joy; He is grace and mercy making us grace and mercy. If all these attributes are invisible and continue to remain that way, the world will not know that the Father does exist and cares immensely for mankind. Because man has come from God, he is absolutely able to hear his Maker. His responsibility then is to respond" (Vishal Jetnarayan: The Nature of the Prophetic)

HIDDEN FIGURES

¹¹ For I know the plans I have for you," declares the Lᴏʀᴅ, "plans to prosper you and not to harm you, plans to give you hope and a future. (Jer.29:11)

God created man in His image and in His likeness. Adam failed in his mission by accepting the lie offered by the enemy instead of the life ordained by his Heavenly Father. As a result of 'the fall' the human race was condemned to death as they lived a life of dysfunction via the alternative satanic vision of what life should be when man is in charge. Even though The Father made accommodations for the reconciliation and redemption of mankind, human beings overwhelmingly choose to continue to eat from the tree of the knowledge of good and evil instead of the tree of life.

I just viewed the movie "Hidden Figures" and was reminded of the unlimited potential of the human soul that is directed by the Spirit of God. How many souls have been denied the opportunity to excel and reach their God given potential because of the fear and prejudice? How many people of every nation are imprisoned by the lie perpetuated by Satan and have no clue who they are? The ministry of reconciliation is the job description of every born again child of God and we are to be the evidence of the kingdom of God in all of our circumstances. It may be decades before the world recognizes God's footprints that were left on this earth when as He walked in and through you. As his sons, our responsibility is to obediently respond to

Him by the power of His Spirit as He lives through us.

When you walk into the LIGHT the darkness will be shattered. Do not spend much time mourning its demise. Accept the truth and the new life that comes with it BY FAITH. Religion is an enemy that keeps us from Life.

WHAT DO YOU WANT TO BE WHEN YOU GROW UP?

This question is easy to answer once you know who you are and why you are here. Children decide who they want to be based on the images they are exposed to during their formative years and beyond. They have hope. As they become older, their aspirations are altered by wants and needs. Materialism replaces spirituality. Ignorance of our true identity perpetuates the drama that ensues and confusion becomes the norm.

Without Christ we are worthless and can produce nothing of eternal value. "In Christ" we are reconciled to our Heavenly Father and have the capacity to manifest His nature by the power of His Spirit. We live by the truth that we are spiritual beings, created in His image, clothed in flesh and designed for His plan and purpose. By faith we are transformed into His likeness as we allow our new selves to be used by Him for His ordained purpose for each of us. Everything else is a distraction.

When your children...when the world sees you, who do they see, you or Jesus?

In order to determine who I want to be I must first know who I am, and that knowledge is impossible to ascertain until I am certain of who God created me to be. (Alex Bess)

"I have been crucified with Christ and I no longer live, but Christ lives in me. The life I now live in the body, I live by faith in the Son of God, who loved me and gave himself for me." (Gal.2:20)

CHECK YOUR EMAIL. Not everything that is addressed to you is for you. Make it your priority to place all of the junk mail into the garbage because that is what it is. Imagine the amount of stress you avoid when you learn to eliminate the mail you receive that has no eternal value and focus only on the that which is a blessing.

WHAT IS FAMILY?

I must admit that the best example of family that I have witnessed is not the church. Because it is next to impossible to locate a human family that does not function out of dysfunction it is also unlikely that the church family can serve as a role model to the world. Our unfamiliarity with the culture of the Kingdom and our failure to be Spirit led in all of our affairs has not helped us to fulfill 'the great commission.' Let's be honest, we do not "love one another as Christ loves us."

The transformation of a disciple of Christ is designed by Almighty God to manifest the character of Christ in and through the believer. The proof of this ongoing process is evidenced by our actions as we fellowship with each other. That fellowship is initiated and orchestrated by the Holy Spirit and inspires and equips us to meet the needs of our family members out of God's love for them through us. As we love each other we become increasingly transparent, less selfish, and totally available for God's plan and purpose and our calling. This is a spiritual reality that should manifest itself in our everyday lives. Because we are aware of our true identity as sons of God we are also aware that our provision and protection are His responsibility and not ours. Because we are aware of His love for us we can focus on loving others. Because we understand that divine love is impossible without a personal relationship with *THE ONE who is love, we also are aware that it is Him who is doing the loving through us and not us. "Love suffers long and is kind; love does not envy; love does not parade itself, is not puffed up; does not behave rudely, does not seek its own, is not provoked, thinks no evil; does not rejoice in iniquity, but rejoices in the truth; bears all things, believes all things, hopes all things, endures all things. LOVE NEVER FAILS." (1 Co.13:4-8)*

When I have a need I call a family member first. Why? Because I know and trust my brothers and my sisters and their God-given gifts are for my benefit. When they bless me they are encouraged by being a blessing and being used by our Father. If I need a carpenter, my brother the carpenter will be my first choice because God will use us to be a blessing to each other. If I need a lawyer, my daughter, the lawyer, will be my first choice. If I need a realtor, my brother the realtor will be my first choice. When these experts are unable to assist, they will refer me to a reliable source. God Himself is loving us when He uses us via our gifts to love each other. Our choices are not difficult when Spirit led. It is only when we are distracted by our own provision and protection that we neglect family and look to the world for what God has already provided.

As new creations "in Christ" and sons of God we have the capacity to manifest the character of Christ in our everyday lives. We can either choose to remain carnal or to allow Christ to live His life through us. The proof of the later is our love for each other. Let's practice what we preach.

CONTAINERS OF GRACE

For the 'born again' Christian new birth means new life. It means that our old life and nature was crucified with Christ on the cross and we are now united with Him in His resurrection. By the power of the Holy Spirit this new creature now has the capacity to manifest the character of

Christ in his/her everyday life. That new life is the life of Christ manifested through the believer by the power of the Holy Spirit and is full of grace and truth.

*"For this cause I Paul, the prisoner of Jesus Christ for you Gentiles, if ye have heard of **the dispensation of the grace of God** which is given to me to you-ward: how that by revelation He made known unto me the mystery;" (Eph.3:1-3)*

We commonly define the grace of God as unmerited favor and thus make ourselves consumers of grace. Like Paul, every son of God is given the ministry of reconciliation and has a specific calling in God's plan and purpose. As we are transformed into the likeness of Christ we are the bringers of grace, the instruments of His grace…the weapons of grace. As Spirit led sons of God we are the **containers of His grace** as He loves others through us. This grace is the power and authority from Almighty God to function as His representatives, His sons in the earth. As His sons, we have the power and authority to speak for God. As He lives through us the world is made aware of The Truth and is convicted of sin.

We cannot compromise our calling as a royal priesthood and a holy nation. Our call NOW is to discard our religion, embrace our relationship with The Father, stop playing church and declare

God's Truth as the Word becomes flesh through us.

"I have been crucified with Christ; it is no longer I who live, but Christ lives in me; and the life which I now live in the flesh I live by faith in the Son of God, who loved me and gave himself for me. I do not set aside the grace of God; for if righteousness comes through the law, then Christ died in vain." (Gal. 2:20-21)

FREEING UP SPACE

My wife's smart phone notified her that because all of the available storage space had been used there would be no more data uploaded or downloaded. No text mails, no voice mails, no nothing. Since I am not an expert in these matters we went to our local provider's store and were informed that downloading Google Photos would solve the problem but first all unnecessary apps would have to be deleted in order to free up some space. Once that was accomplished the 3000+ photos stored on her phone could be transferred into the cloud via the new app.

There are two kinds of people. Those who have been deceived by and continue to live the lie while rejecting the absolute Truth of the Word of

God are full of useless data as it relates to eternal life. Unlike my wife's phone they still receive and send out useless worldly information that has no eternal value. These daily transactions serve to secure provision and protection by natural means. When that is not the objective their time is filled with distractions that serve the purpose of entertaining the human soul. Those who have heard and accepted the Truth of the gospel of the kingdom have been 'born again' and by faith are 'new creations in Christ.' These souls have been declared righteous and perfect and secure because of their relationship with Almighty through His Son, Jesus. In their new life all the space has been freed up for the acquisition and manifestation of the character of Christ. The old useless aps are being deleted as the process of transformation allows the filling of the Spirit day by day, moment by moment.

As sons of God we have access to unlimited data as we are transformed into the image of Christ and equipped to attain our full potential as perfect representatives of our Heavenly Father.

THE REALITY OF SONSHIP

According to the gospel of Matthew Jesus was baptized by John the Baptist. It was an event which shows us the trinity in action as the Holy Spirit, in the form of a dove, settles upon Jesus and God the Father speaks from heaven and says, "*This is my beloved Son, in whom I am well pleased." (Mt. 3:17)* Immediately after this astonishing scene the Son of God is then led by the Spirit into the wilderness to be tempted by the devil.

The drama we experience in life can be traced to one of two sources. Those who have not accepted the Truth of the gospel suffer from perpetual dysfunction and survive by their own attempts at provision and protection. They consistently eat from the forbidden tree of the knowledge of good and evil and put absolutely no trust in The sovereign Father who loves them. Those who have submitted to the gospel of the kingdom are not exempt from drama but are not affected adversely. We have eternal life. Our provision and protection is guaranteed by our Heavenly Father and as we learn to operate in love we also learn to rejoice in our sufferings. Our life is focused on the ministry of reconciliation directed and empowered by the Holy Spirit. *"For as many as are led by the Spirit of God, they are the sons of God." (Rom. 8:14)*

As sons of God we are one with Christ and worthy as persons. Our union with Christ allows us to function in both the temporal and eternal. By faith, we accept the truth of what God has done for us that we could not do for ourselves. We believe not only that God is who He says He is but that we are who He says we are and we enter into the fullness of the gospel of Jesus Christ in our daily lives. _We are one with Christ and we are in Him and He is in us. We are loved unconditionally (Eph.2:1-10), totally accepted (Eph. 1:3-6), forever forgiven (Col.2:9-15), totally accepted (Eph. 1:3-6), forever forgiven (Col. 2:9-15), important as ambassadors (2 Co. 5:17-21), meaningful in ministry (Jn.14:12), and adequate in power (Phil. 4:13)._ As Christ lives through us we are assured by the same words that were spoken of Jesus after His baptism…"This is my beloved son, in whom I am well pleased."

LOVE, TIME, DEATH

"Collateral Beauty" is one of the best movies I have viewed in a long time but was released too late to be considered for an award. It is infinitely better than the movie that was the academy award winner. The movie features Will Smith as the majority owner of a marketing firm that is a victim of his depression suffered through the death of his six year old daughter. It begins with his speech to the firms employees about the abstract concepts of love, time, and death and how every relationship (and marketing success) is based on these three entities. We all have a desire to love and be loved; we are all running out of time; we are all afraid of death.

These three 'truths' are viewed from a worldly perspective and Mr. Smith's misunderstanding of the relationship between the three and how they affect human nature yields surprising results by the end of the movie. Our 'understanding' of the world around us is insufficient to discern the truth of situations and circumstances without an eternal perspective. In fact, in order to initiate an awareness of God's eternal truth about who He is and who we are He must first appeal to our flesh. At some point in our lives, either as a last resort or as an attempt to increase our worldly position, we choose religion as a last resort rather than a personal relationship with The Father.

The church today focuses its attention on messages and programs that accommodate social justice, the gospel of prosperity, and a religion that rewards us with a heaven that holds all the benefits of our faith in escrow until after we pass away. Ironically, the appeal to our flesh is only successful as a result of our own desperation or as a result of failing to secure our own provision and protection. Our ignorance concerning who God created us to be is our normal state. However, most Christians are still unaware of who they are 'in Christ' and fail to experience the transformation afforded by the power and presence of the Holy Spirit. Their pre-occupation with their own provision and protection is the result of unbelief and a lack of complete trust in a Sovereign Father who loves them.

As we allow the life of Christ to be manifested through us as new creations "in Christ" we are transformed into mature sons of God who manifest His character and nature as He loves through us. Time is not important because physical death is the beginning of new life in eternity. *"But we all, with unveiled face, beholding as in a mirror the glory of the Lord, are being transformed into the same image from glory to glory, just as by the Spirit of the Lord."*

PERFECT LOVE

God is love. The nature of His being is the definition of perfect love. Since He is love anything other than the manifestation of His nature cannot be referred to as love. Therefore, there is no such thing as imperfect love. Love is not love unless God is doing the loving.

Rev. 12:11 speaks of a holy nation, a royal priesthood, a people who, with their backs against the wall, have persevered and conquered Satan by the blood of the Lamb and the word of their testimony. They understood that they could not live by God's perfect standard (the Law) and surrendered their lives to the Truth of the gospel and allowed Christ to live His life through them. They did not share the confusion of the young lawyer who asked Jesus to clarify his understanding of the greatest commandment. *"You shall love the Lord your God with all your heart and with all your soul and with all your mind. This is the great and first commandment. And a second is like it: You shall love your neighbor as yourself. On these two commandments depend all the Law and the Prophets." (Mt.22:37-40)* Jesus quoted the law which required that we do the best we can with all that we have to love God first above everything else and then love our brother as we love ourselves. Both are impossibilities when we are operating according to the flesh. Both are impossible without the nature of God via the power of the indwelling Spirit.

How were these overcomers in Rev.12:11 prepared by The Father to stand and conquer? They were given a new commandment. *"A new commandment I give to you, that you love one another: just as I have love you, you also are to love one another. By this all people will know that you are my disciples, if you have love for one another." (Jn.13:34-35)* This new commandment was the same as the old commandment but was qualified by the phrase "as I have loved you". Jesus was the perfect representation of The Father and He loved us more than He loved His own life. He loved us with a perfect love and by the power of the Holy Spirit in us we are to love each other perfectly. *"You therefore must be perfect, as your heavenly Father is perfect." (Mt.5:48…43-48)*

As partakers of His divine nature (2 Pt.1:3-4) we are equipped to manifest the character of Christ in our everyday lives in a way that identifies us as sons of God and **THE STANDARD FOR PERFECT LOVE IS THE SAME FOR MAN AS IT IS FOR GOD.**

ENEMIES OF THE FAITH

"Be kindly affectionate to one another with brotherly love, in honor giving preference to one another; not lagging in diligence, fervent in spirit, serving the Lord; rejoicing in hope, patient in tribulation, continuing steadfastly in prayer, distributing to the needs of the saints, given to hospitality." (Rom.12:10)
EMEMIES OF THE FAITH

You may already be aware of the fact that the common enemies of the faith are THE WORLD, the FLESH, and the DEVIL. Most believers will agree with this conclusion even when they continue to struggle with one or more of these enemies.

It is obvious that **"the thief comes only to steal and kill and destroy" (Jn.10:10).** The word of God instructs us **to "Put on the whole armor of God, that you may be able to stand against the schemes of the devil. For we do not wrestle against flesh and blood, but against the rulers, against the authorities, against the cosmic powers over this present darkness, against the spiritual forces of evil in the heavenly places" (Eph.6:11-12)**. Satan is the father of lies and his greatest lie is that he does not exist. He destroys both lives and relationships by convincing us that we are in charge of our own lives and are equipped to accomplish that task on our own.

Life in the FLESH originates from the selfish desires of the soul. The abuse of the gift of free will results in choices made without the benefit of divine knowledge. A life not guided by the Holy Spirit is doomed to destruction and is worthless in regard to God's eternal plan and purpose for mankind. **"Anyone who does not have the Spirit of Christ does not belong to Him. But if Christ is in you, although the body is dead because of sin, the Spirit is life because of righteousness. If the Spirit of Him who raised Jesus from the dead dwells in you, He who raised Christ Jesus from the dead will also give life to your mortal bodies through His Spirit who dwells in you" (Rom.8:9-11).**

The failure of the 1st Adam to obey God resulted in his God-given dominion authority being transferred to Satan. His separation from The Father made personal provision and protection the priority for a life of selfishness and sin. Satan's provision for the satisfaction of this dilemma was the WORLD, composed of systems designed to accommodate the illusion of attainable worthiness without God. Man depends on and lives by the false assumption that "I will be worthy if…" That statement is completed by some temporary solution to an eternal issue that requires a spiritual perspective. For that reason the result can only be the further development of the insanity initiated by the lie called the world. **"Do not love** the world or the things in the world. I anyone loves the world, the love of the Father is not in him. For all that is in the world—the desires of the flesh and the desires of the eyes and pride of life—is not from the Father but is from the world " (1 Jn.2:15-16).

The mature believer can only become useful and affective in the body of Christ when he/she recognizes the final enemy…RELIGION. Through our identification with Christ in both His death and resurrection we are no longer under law but under grace. We no longer strive for perfection because we are perfect "in Christ". His righteousness is now what clothes us. This is what the celebration of Easter is all about…Rom. 8:1-6

THE THIRD DAY

"Now Jesus, going up to Jerusalem, took the twelve disciples aside on the road and said to them, 'Behold, we are going up to Jerusalem, and the Son of Man will be betrayed to the chief priests and to the scribes; and they will condemn Him to death, and deliver Him to the Gentiles to mock and to scourge and to crucify. **And the third day He will rise again."** (Mt.20:17-19)

As we approach the celebration of the resurrection of The Savior we are reminded of what He suffered for our sake. His trial, humiliation, and death on the cross are more than any of us will ever suffer. It is easy to view the story and then put it away until we are forced to review the facts twelve months from now. Most of us will spend maybe 3 or 4 of the 168 hours that compose our week showing our appreciation for what Jesus did for us that we could not do for ourselves. To be honest, most of us do not live as if we believe the words of Paul when he said: *"I have been crucified with Christ; it is no longer I who live, but Christ lives in me; and the life which I now live in the flesh I live by faith in the Son of God,* **who loved me and gave Himself for me."** *(Gal. 2:20)*

The celebration of the resurrection of our Lord and Savior, like most religious holidays, has been tainted by eggs laid by a rabbit and a fashion show. The world's celebration of "Easter" is mostly about the bottom line and not the ultimate sacrifice that led to redemption and salvation. Every child of God has the capacity to manifest the resurrected life of Christ moment-by-moment. The Spirit led life is a constant reminder of the fact that for the Christian "Easter" is every day. *"For if we have been united together in the likeness of His death, certainly we also shall be in* **the likeness of His resurrection***, knowing this, that our old man was crucified with Him, that the body of* *sin might be done away with, that we should no longer be slaves to sin. For he who has died has been freed from sin." (Rom.6:5-7)*

HAPPY RESURRECTION DAY...EVERY DAY.

DIET & EXERCISE

Most doctors will agree that good physical health is not possible without a good diet and regular exercise. We usually only think of the word 'diet' as relating to the need to decrease our caloric intake, change what and when we eat, and hopefully alter our physical image. Nutritionist will inform you that many of the foods we eat are killing us. Profit, and not proper nutrition, is the goal of major food chains and we find ourselves deceived by labels, additives, and marketing strategies. The things that should be part of our normal diet are usually the things we were not introduced to during our formative years. We love junk food and anything that contains sugar must be good. Even when we are informed of the dangers presented by the things we have grown to love our addiction to those sustainers of the health industry is difficult to overcome.

The blessing of technology has also become a curse in that it has made us lazy. Be honest! The two groups of people who exercise regularly, over and above what would be considered normal, are those for whom it has been prescribed and those who have become addicted to it. At any rate, our love of the body has expanded an industry designed to provide false hope for our lack of discipline and our ignorance of who we truly are.

We all have needs but we are not normally aware of the scope of those needs. As triune beings made in the image of God we cannot reach our full potential until our spiritual needs (the need to love others as Christ loved us) are met. Our spiritual health should be our first priority but can only be address once our physical and personal needs are met. Jesus is the only answer when it comes to meeting ALL our needs.

A personal relationship with The Father through our union with Jesus insures a healthy spirit. A steady diet of God's Word, prayer, faith in His promises and the application (exercise) of the knowledge of His truth in our lives results in us trusting in Him for our provision and protection while we become Christ to others.

A SPIRIT LED LIFE IS A HEALTHY LIFE.

As you attempt to manage the lives of those around you remember, your efforts will not be welcomed or appreciated until you learn how to manage your own.

LOOKING GOOD

*"For whom He foreknew, He also **predestined to be conformed to the image of His Son**, that He might be the firstborn among many brethren."* (Rom.8:29)

The world we live in equates 'looking good' to physical appearance. The health and beauty industry makes billions from those products that promise to enhance the physical presentation of the human body to comply with society's standard for beauty. Makeup and hair have become necessities for most females, not to mention the proper seasonal apparel. Products of every kind are marketed to appeal to our emotions as inanimate identities that enhance our own.

This is the world standard by which we were raised and both normal and natural for every living soul. But, the truth will set you free. It is only through a personal relationship with our Heavenly Father that we can know ourselves and shed the illusion of 'looking good' as an external attribute. The internal beauty of our union with Christ results in the manifestation of His character and the nature of Almighty God…the nature of love. True beauty emanates from a quickened spirit and shines through our external housing.

LOOKING GOOD is about being conformed into the image of Christ. Once we realize that ALL of our needs are met 'in Christ' we are then free to fulfill our God-given destiny of being Christ to others and loving as He does. Next time you check out how good you look do not look for a mirror. Look into His Word to see yourself and then take a spiritual 'selfie.' You are not looking good until your Father looks at you and sees His Son. Every other evaluation is a waste of time.

THE AVERAGE CHRISTIAN

Are you an average Christian? I hope not. There is nothing average about the true Christian. There is nothing average about being united with Christ, empowered by the Holy Spirit, and privileged with being an ambassador of Christ through a personal relationship with the sovereign King of the universe.

The average Christian:
Never led anyone to Christ
Never read the entire bible
Is a silent witness
Only attends church on Sundays…sometimes
Looks like everyone else
Acts like everyone else
Has no idea of their purpose
Has no clue of their true identity
Is not actively involved in their God-given ministry
Talks much—prays little

New birth means new life. As new creations 'in Christ' we are empowered and authorized to represent the King of the universe through the ministry of reconciliation. Our #1 priority is to 'be Christ' to others in ALL our actions. There is nothing average about the 'great commission.'

"Now then, we are ambassadors for Christ, as though God were pleading through us: we implore you on Christ's behalf, be reconciled to God. For He made Him who knew no sin to be sin for us, that we might become the righteousness of God in Him." (2 Co.5:20)

A BROTHERLY & ORDERLY LIFE

"But we urge you, brethren, that you increase more and more; 'that you also <u>aspire to lead a quiet life</u>, to mind your own business, and to work with your own hands, as we commanded you, that you may walk properly toward those who are outside, and that you may lack nothing." (1 Thes.4:10-12)

Shut up! Give up! Grow up! Get up & go!

Death and life are in the power of the tongue (Prov.18:21). We must learn to refrain from offering our opinions of situations and circumstances that are not in agreement with God's Word. Say what God says. If you are not a conduit for His conversation…*<u>SHUT UP!</u>*

Hopelessness is a reality only for those who reject Christ. Our commitment to His plan and purpose requires complete trust in Him. Our trust is evidenced by our willingness to stop trying to take charge of our lives and the lives of others and let Him speak through us... *GIVE UP!*

Spiritual growth is evidenced by the manifestation of the nature and character of Christ in the believer. Your personal growth is in direct proportion to your commitment to God's Truth...*GROW UP!*

Love is not passive. The goal of the transformation process is for us to 'be Christ' to others. This is only possible via the presence and power of the Holy Spirit as we are led into the fulfillment or our ordained destinies...*GET UP AND GO!*

I am still learning how to 'shut up.' The rest of the journey becomes easier as I learn how to keep quiet and listen to His voice. My spiritual growth excels as I actively 'get up and go' and apply His truth to the life He has ordained for me. Instead of listening to myself or the opinions of others I am learning to 'shut up' and filter everything through His Word so that my response will sound like Him and my actions will look like His. I am learning that true life is 'giving up' all of me so that I can attain ALL of Him.

BUCKET LIST (Phil.3:10)

Many people have formulated a list of things they want to do before they die. The trouble is that most people have waited too late to accomplish all the things on their list or discovered that the cost of some items was out of their range of finances. If you were asked about the things you would like to accomplish before you leave this earth what would your list look like?

Here is a consideration. If you are a born again Christian, would your list look any different now than it would if you had composed it before you were redeemed? You may not agree with me but I am under the impression that my bucket list should consist of only one item based on Paul's letter to the church at Phillipi. *"I count all things to be loss for the excellency of the knowledge of Christ Jesus my Lord: for whom I suffered the loss of all things, and do count them but refuse, that I may gain Christ, and be found in Him, not having a righteousness of mine own, even that which is of the law, but that which is through faith in Christ, the righteousness which is from God by faith*: <u>that I may know Him, and the power of His resurrection, and the fellowship of His sufferings, becoming conformed unto</u>

His death; if by any means I may attain unto the resurrection from the dead.(Phil.3:8-11)

PROGRAMMED FOR IGNORANCE

"All scripture is given by inspiration of God, and is profitable for doctrine, for reproof, for correction, for instruction in righteousness, that the man of God may be complete, thoroughly equipped for every good work."
(2 Tim.3:16)

It is possible to be successful according to the world's standard while failing in life. Our quest for information is both challenging and useless when measured by its eternal value. Our innate selfishness prevents us from becoming a true blessing to those who may receive temporary benefits from our efforts.

All truth begins with scripture. All knowledge is incomplete unless filtered through God's Holy Word. Man's efforts to perfect his own righteousness will never end in peace and harmony. It is the righteousness of Christ we must seek and it is a free gift to all who will accept the Gospel. Until a man knows who God is, he will never know who he is. Without an intentional submission to the Word of God and the life of Christ we will remain ignorant of the

114

truth that sets men free. A constant and consistent ingestion of the knowledge of the world leaves us ignorant of the Truth. Without the power and discernment of the Holy Spirit and the truth of the Word of God we are programmed for ignorance.

If you don't know Jesus…you don't know nothing!"

FOCUS

You cannot look directly into the sun, but you also cannot see anything without it. It is impossible to focus in the dark. *"He has delivered us from the power of darkness and conveyed us into the kingdom of the Son of His love, in whom we have redemption through His blood, the forgiveness of sins."* (Col.1:13-14)

BOLDNESS (a prayer)

Heavenly Father, you are Almighty God. You made the heavens and earth and every thing that is in them. You spoke everything into existence and without you nothing can exist. Men deny your mercy, grace, and existence.

Men still elect to eat from the tree of the knowledge of good and evil. All men have sinned and come short of your glory.

You have shown mercy and given grace to those who receive your truth and your love. As your sons we have wisdom and discernment. We see the world through your eyes. I pray that we will cease from groaning and complaining about things we refuse to confront with the truth of the gospel. I pray that we will not be distracted by social, political, and personal issues that have no effect whatsoever on our eternal salvation. I pray that we would realize that in Christ ALL our needs are met and that we are free to love others as Christ loves us. Grant, Father, that your sons will speak your Word only WITH BOLDNESS and that our conversations would be the manifestation of the character of Christ in us. Stretch out your hand and heal. Use us for your glory and do signs and wonders. IN THE NAME OF JESUS I pray.

Imagine missionaries going to New Guinea. They're there to love the cannibals. Things are tough and the native peoples are against them, but they keep rejoicing. One day, two tribesmen hit them with rocks and the missionaries forget that they're missionaries. It's no longer a mission field- it's home. That's exactly how it is for most believers. They treat the world as home and forget that it's really a mission field. Most believers live their lives as missionaries with amnesia. We forget that we're here on a mission and think that we're here to survive or get by, to get the most out of it, to fit in, be successful, or impress people. We care what people think of us. But we're not here for that. We're here to give and be a witness and to shine our lights into the darkness. Stop trying to fit in with the cannibals to become a successful cannibal. Wake up! You're not at home and you're not hanging out, you're here to bless. This is your mission field! So get on with your mission. Everything else is just a bad case of amnesia. (author unknown)

SPIRITUAL GROWTH

There are three kinds of people in the world. There are those who complain about the condition of the world and want to see change that will make things better for themselves. There are those who want to change the world to conform to their idea of what utopia should look like. And, there are those who have come to the realization that the world will not change until they do. These are the 'called out' ones. Those that fall into the last category also realize that without Christ, change is impossible. What category are you in?

Without the benefit of God's divine wisdom and the revelation of His truth it is impossible to make justifiable decisions about anything. Before we receive the truth of the Word of God we are slaves of the dominion of darkness and all our decisions are made in the dark. Our incomplete knowledge of a matter leads us to an emotional commitment to unrighteous (or self-righteous) conclusions based on false assumptions. It is only when we are delivered into the kingdom of light that we can see the light and then be the light for others.

God's intention is to raise up a holy nation and a royal priesthood. The family of God grows as personal decisions are made to submit to the guidance and direction of the Holy Spirit. As 'new creations' we are commissioned ambassadors for

Christ and are called out to represent Him in EVERYTHING we say and do. ***Have you made the decision to submit to that transformation process or are you still just going to church?***

BLIND AMBITION

"Where there is no prophetic vision the people cast off restraint, but blessed is he who keeps the law." (Proverbs 29:18)

AMBITION is defined as a strong desire to do or to achieve something, typically requiring determination and hard work. It is not difficult to recognize the ambitious efforts of every segment of the world in which we live. From the single efforts of an individual to the intentional struggling of national leaders, the ambitious goals of a people are expressed and promoted. When we fail to achieve our stated goals, we pick ourselves up and proclaim that 'we can be great again.'

The sad truth is that this same attitude is evident in many of our churches. Individual dreams and desires are promoted and supported for the purpose of building bigger buildings, increasing membership, and celebrating accomplishments that may even benefit others but are the product of the flesh. *We have replaced VISION with ambition* and are too blind to recognize this. Not only have we failed to see the kingdom, we have failed to enter the kingdom because we are too busy *doing without trusting*. JESUS DID NOT COME TO DO GOOD WORKS. JESUS CAME TO SHOW US THE FATHER.

As individual members of the corporate Body of Christ we must let the light in us shine through us. Our commission to 'GO' is for the purpose of Christ using us to reveal Himself to the world and the light that dispels the darkness. Through me and you and us, the world must not just see our ambitious attempts to do good; the world must see the fulfillment of His vision for us...the world must see Christ in us. The sons of God are called to BE CHRIST to others in the power of the Spirit. (Acts 2:17)

THE WALKING DEAD

According to Romans 6 my natural life ended when I
accepted the Truth of the Gospel of the Kingdom
which informs me that when Jesus was crucified on
the cross, so was I. The penalty that He paid for the
sins of man when He shed His blood covered me and
you, past, present, and future. He was raised from
the dead and is now King of kings and Lord of lords
and by the power of the Holy Spirit that same
resurrection power and authority lives in and
through me as a new creation "in Christ." According
to Rom. 8:1 *'there is now no condemnation for
those who are in Christ Jesus'* and I can now consider
myself dead to sin and alive to God.

In addition to the witness of the Spirit to my spirit
that I am now a son of God, this truth is evidenced
through the life that Christ now lives in and through
me. *"Therefore, if anyone is in Christ, he is a new
creation. The old has passed away; behold, the new
has come. This is from God, who through Christ
reconciled us to himself and gave us the ministry of
reconciliation." (2 Co.2:17-18)* As an ambassador for
Christ, I am sent into the world with His authority

and power with the commission to make disciples by submitting to the guidance and direction of the Holy Spirit as I am used by God to show to those still in darkness, The Father. He uses me and you to fulfill His promise of sonship and we get to share in His glory. Can it get any better than that?

The Scriptures describe death as separation from Almighty God, The Father. If you are not GROWING, in His grace, you're one of the walking dead. **You are either growing or dying**. The choice is yours.

FAMILY

Now here is a word that we have failed to understand. Webster offers its definition as: the basic unit in society traditionally consisting of two parents rearing their children; also: any of various social units differing from but regarded as equivalent to the traditional **family** a single-parent **family**. This definition is not only secular, which makes it acceptable to the general public, but dysfunctional.

FAMILY was God's idea. The first picture of the family in the Bible is the Trinity. The Father's creation of man, and then woman, and His instruction to be fruitful and multiply was intended to establish the family that would represent the Trinity. The truly functional family is one that represents God the Father, Son and Holy Spirit in the earth.

With this in mind, the correct way to spell 'family' is LOVE. It is impossible to manifest God's concept of 'family' without the character and nature of God, who is Love. This means that each individual family member puts himself/herself last and loves the others 'as Christ.' The LOVE that we show each other is **patient and kind.** _"Love does not envy or boast; it is not arrogant or rude. It does not insist on its own way; it is not irritable or resentful; it does not rejoice at wrongdoing,"_ (1 Co.13:4-6) Family (LOVE) is impossible without the presence of The Holy Spirit as the life of the believer.

One needs to remember that family (LOVE) _"rejoices with the truth; bears all things, believes all things, hopes all things, endures all things. LOVE NEVER FAILS."_ (1 Co.13:7-8) The dysfunctional status of the human family can only be reversed by the 'new birth' of the believer into the family of God. What does your 'family' look like? What do you look like to them?

LOVE ONE ANOTHER

If you claim to be a child of God...an ambassador for Christ...and your actions do not reflect the character and nature of your Heavenly Father, you are confusing others. Our transformation is designed to result in us becoming the exact representation of The Father.

STOP worrying about what others say about you...God's opinion is the only one that counts. **STOP** complaining about where you are in life...if you have a mind and two feet you can always leave.
STOP criticizing and slandering others because they don't see and do things the way you do...your assessment of wrong is proven to not be right if the thing to be done is completed. **STOP** trying to control and manipulate others. Regardless of your motive, you have never achieved self-control.

 ENCOURAGE others by believing for them and have the patience to let them fail. It is the best lesson that they could learn. Their full potential (and yours) can only be reached "in Christ."
SEE OTHERS as God sees them and not according to the flesh...then let Him speak thru you.

LOVE never fails. Hate is the poison that people take when they fail to control others. If you elect to talk about each other instead of to each other, remember that if there is nothing good to say, don't say anything. What is being said about you?

"A new commandment I give to you, that you love one another; just as I have loved you, you also are to love one another. By this all people will know that you are my disciples, if you have love for one another." (Jn.13:34-35)

The Stages of Sonship

Nepios...

We are afforded the blessing of salvation via death and resurrection. Once we receive the gospel we are made new "in Christ" and adopted into the family of God. We are now sons of God...a royal priesthood and a holy nation. Since God is the Father of our spirits, and spirits have no gender, we are all sons.

The first stage of sonship is 'nepios'. This is a baby Christian and like all babies is helpless and ignorant. Baby Christians need care and nurture because they have absolutely no knowledge of situation or circumstance and no training. As new born babes they are not mature enough to handle the resources of the household. Their reactions are founded in an innate curiosity about the world around them. Their actions originate from either a loaded diaper or an empty bottle. They need to be both fed and changed since they are incapable of doing either. They are emotional and selfish and cry when they do not get their way. Proper growth requires the commitment of others who are willing to meet their needs because of their love for them and not out of a just sense of duty. When you care for babies you have to be conscience of both your actions and your conversation. New borns are sensitive to both. Babies who are raised and nurtured by those who rule according to the law and not by grace grow up to be just like those who raised them.

"For though by this time you ought to be teachers, you have need again for someone to teach you the elementary principles of the oracles of God, and you have come to need milk and not solid food. For everyone who partakes only of milk is not accustomed to the word of righteousness, for he is an infant (nepios). But solid food is for the mature,

who because of practice have their senses trained to discern good and evil (Heb.5:12-14)"

As new born Christians, all of us have experienced this stage of sonship. We are not, however, expected to remain in this stage until Jesus returns.

Paidion/Teknon

"I am writing to you, fathers, because you know Him who has been from the beginning. I am writing to you, young men (neaniskos), because you have overcome the evil one. I have written to you, children (paidion), because you know the Father (1 Jn.2:13)

As new born babies grow they, at some point, enter the second stage of sonship called the **paidion** stage. These little children can now recognize the Father but are still, for all practical purposes, infants. Even though they may be able to feed themselves and have graduated to pull-ups they are still messy and have to be kept under close supervision.

As these sons continue to mature they reach the stage called **teknon**. They now are capable of assuming limited responsibility and are tasked with the opportunity to respond to rule. This may be difficult for some depending on the guidance and care they received in the beginning stages. These 'teens' tend to assume that they have a grasp of the complete knowledge of the world and seldom fail to express these feelings. They are active without purpose and prone to make mistakes. The discipline needed to facilitate their growth must be consistent and uncompromising. They will not always understand the love that dictates this process. The **teknon** is a son who is sufficiently mature to engage a reciprocal relationship with the Father.

"A man had two sons, and he came to the first and said, 'Son, go work today in the vineyard.' And he answered, 'I will not'; but afterward he regretted it and went. The man came to the second and said the same thing; and he answered, 'I will, sir': but he did not go. Which of the two did the will of his father?" They said, 'the first." Jesus said to them, "Truly I say to you that the tax collectors and prostitutes will get into the kingdom of God before you." (Mt. 21:28-31)

Sons who are mature enough to be given rule and responsibility but are inconsistent if complying to the will of their father need more training before they are acceptable as sons who can facilitate the complete representation of their father. In many ways the teknon is still a child.

Neaniskos / Huios

In the process of transformation a son who has been tested and has overcome and represented the word of God is in the stage called 'neaniskos.' This son is no longer a child and has overcome the enemy through suffering...1 Jn. 2:13-15

The final stage of sonship is called 'huios'. This is the son who can be used by God as a full representation of His character and nature. This is a true son who is directed and led by the Holy Spirit. This son can be observed in the parable in Matthew 21:33-44. This is the son who is sent to represent the Father in the power of the Holy Spirit to establish the standards of righteousness via his representation.

As sons of God we all go through each of these stages. Our awareness of the transformation process and our faith in what God is doing to and through us by the power of His Holy Spirit will allow us to persevere and submit to His plan and purpose for our lives. Our destiny is to glorify Him as sons in every area of the life He lives through us. WHERE ARE YOU IN THIS PROCESS?

UNANSWERED QUESTIONS...

I grew up during a time when the term 'blind faith' meant that you must accept not only the answers offered by the church relating to the Word of God, but you must also accept the explanation for your unanswered questions. That explanation was that some answers are not available on this side of heaven. Then I read that God has reveled to us through His Spirit (1 Co. 2:10) everything we need to know to fulfill our destiny. So why is it that we spend so much time 'in the dark' once we are saved? Maybe the church does not have the answers to our questions. Maybe we are asking the wrong questions. Maybe we don't trust God to reveal to us the information we need to be who He has designed us to be. Maybe we don't want to know the answers. If you are serious about your spiritual growth here are some questions you need to be asking for your own personal growth.

What comes before "In the beginning..." and the creation of the heavens and the earth?

What was God's purpose for creating mankind and what was His intent for them?

What did the culture of man look like during the 930 years that Adam was king of the earth?

Is the church today fulfilling its' purpose according to God's original intent?

Am I, as a believer, fulfilling my purpose according to God's intent for my life?

If the truth will set you free, do I know, or want to know, the whole truth?

What is the culture of an orphan?

What is the culture of a son of God.

How can I get the answers to these and all the other questions I have about God's truth?

If you are satisfied with your present level of spiritual growth and content in your faith, may God continue to bless you. If this is not the case we invite you to contact us. Maybe we can help.

Alex/ Dominion Ministries Inc. /
dominionpreacher@gmail.com

CLARITY...

I recently viewed a commercial for a product that claims to change the way you see the world. Because sunlight creates conditions that hide the beauty of the island of Maui, these sunglasses are reported to provide the color, clarity and detail that escape our natural vision. Maui Jim sunglasses have solved that problem and for an average of $300 you can experience the clarity they provide.

Newsflash.....the sun is NOT the cause of our lack of clarity. Man was designed by God to receive revelation, understanding and clarity directly from God in his spirit. The soul distorts what is seen in the natural because of the lack of divine revelation that is only available to those who have received the 'new life' provided by the death and resurrection of Jesus. It is the sacrifice of the SON and the presence of the Spirit that changes the way we see the world around us and this vision correction has already been paid for.

BLIND FAITH

The faith we are all familiar with can be described as blind faith. It is that faith that operates in darkness. It is that faith that is rooted in a worldly perspective of everything and everyone we encounter and is the result of our personal limited knowledge of good and evil. Blind faith is about as reliable as dumb luck.

As sons of God we have the advantage of revelation knowledge. As new creations "in Christ" we exist in both the natural realm and the eternal realm simultaneously and have the privilege of viewing things through God's eyes. The light that is in us shines through us as we serve as a holy nation and a royal priesthood in a dark and dysfunctional world. We are no longer blinded by the evil one and the clarity that the Spirit provides enables us to 'be Christ' to others.

"Eye has not seen, nor ear heard. Nor have entered into the heart of man the things which God has prepared for those who love Him. **But God has revealed them to us through His Spirit**. For the Spirit *searches all things, yes, the deep things of God."* (1 Co.2:9-10)

CONTENTMENT

"Now **godliness** with **contentment** is great gain, for we brought nothing into the world, and we cannot take anything out of the world." (1 Tim. 6:6-7)

As sons of God we have the privilege of taking ALL our concerns to The Sovereign Father of the universe who has ALL the answers. Because of our faith and trust in His love for us we need not grumble, complain, or criticize anyone or anything. God is in control and Romans 8:28 is still true. **True contentment is reserved for the sons of God.**

As we are transformed into the image of Christ the character and nature of God is manifested in and through us. That's godliness in action. Contentment may be defined as our acceptance of God's will in our lives. It is a learned response and is beyond our natural abilities. It is the life of Christ manifested through us (Phil.4:13; Gal.2:20). It is inseparable from the peace that surpasses ALL understanding (Jn.14:27)

As we yield to the direction of the Holy Spirit we reflect His peace and become the proof that we are right with God because our mind is turned to Him and not on ourselves. Everything we say and do should not only be Spirit led but a statement of God's truth in a dark world. Our conversation, witness, lifestyle, and testimony should reflect the character of Christ and not the feelings and opinion of the natural man. Our actions should be grounded in what we believe and not how we feel. May I challenge you to remember this truth the next time you engage in a discussion or decide to post on the internet. The opinion of your natural man can only bring more dysfunction and not life. Express your content with God's plan and purpose. Be satisfied (content) with who God has made you to be and what He has given you. Be the light. Pray for those who are still blinded by the evil one and then love the hell out of them.

TRUE LIFE

We often spend so much time trying to live that we miss out on LIFE. Our concept of life is limited by our worldly perspective and motivated by the desires of the flesh. It is a product of the soul and even when it yields temporary satisfaction its ensuing drama always ends in death...emotionally, socially, relationally, and physically.

True life can only be experienced by those who discover and submit to the Truth of the Word of God. This is the life of Christ manifested in and through the believer. It is the life reserved for the sons of God who are used by The Father for His plan and purpose. ***TRUE LIFE IS CHRIST.***

CONVERSATIONS

Our conversations are defined not only by what we say but by how we live. They reveal who we are and where we are as it relates to our spiritual growth. We all experience stages of transformation that are evidenced via of our conversation. Regardless of our education or intellect we function as babes without the benefit of revelation knowledge. Both non-believers and new believers are identified by a conversation devoid of understanding. Like parrots, babies can only repeat what they have heard from others. They are threatened by questions which require them to explain their answers.

The second stage of conversation is exhibited by those (paidion/teknon) whose transformation reveals an intellectual understanding devoid of the discipline that comes with full maturity. Their conversation is full of opinions and conclusions derived from their own interpretation of right and wrong. Their boldness is a result of false assumptions made concerning their provision, protection and significance. They have an incomplete knowledge of the gospel and find it difficult to put their complete trust in The Father who loves them. They are like preachers who prepare their own sermons and then search for a scripture to support it.

Mature sons of God practice what they preach. They are not distracted by conversations that distract them from their calling as ambassadors for Christ. They function as a holy nation and a royal priesthood. They are often misunderstood by those who don't speak the kingdom language (love).

JUDGING OTHERS

"Judge not, that you be not judged. For with the judgment you pronounce you will be judged, and with the measure you use it will be measured to you." (Mt. 7:1-2)

Our misconception of this scripture causes many problems. No man is qualified to judge another man because 'we all have sinned and come short of the glory of God". In the flesh we make judgments about others based on our own selfish opinions. Judgment implies a final decision made based on worldly information devoid of spiritual revelation. On the basis of what we have heard, what we see, or what we think we make decisions (judgments) about people we don't even know without consideration of who they are or what they are going through. On that basis, even when we are right we are wrong. Only God has the right to judge what He has made.

The sons of God have a unique advantage…. discernment. Because we have the advantage of revelation knowledge our perception of others is Spirit led and we are allowed to see what God sees. This gives us the ability to be used by The Father to minister rather than manipulate. In the flesh we ask questions about others that reflect how an encounter or relationship may affect us personally.

Our selfish concerns are the priority. In the Spirit we ask only for guidance and direction on how to minister to the other person. We don't judge. We are used by God to inform, teach and encourage and love. This kind of ministry may not always be received or appreciated and may even be considered as judgement. However, as sons of God we are the vessels that The Father uses for His plan and purpose. We are equipped to "be Christ to others."

THE NORMAL CHRISTIAN LIFE...

God has only one answer to every human need—His Son Christ Jesus. He died instead of us for our forgiveness; He lives instead of us for our deliverance. So we have two substitutions: a Substitute on the Cross who secures our forgiveness and a Substitute within who secures our victory.

"The common conception of sanctification is that every item of our life should be holy; but that it not holiness—it is the *fruit* of holiness. Holiness is *Christ*.

When we are conscious of pride, we think that humility will meet our need; but the answer to pride is not humility—it is **Christ**, and Christ is the answer to **every** need. God will not give you humility or patience or love as separate gifts of His grace; He has given you Christ, and if you simply trust Him to live out His life in you, He will be humble, patient, loving and everything else that you need, in your stead. God is not a retailer; He does not deal out grace to us in doses. He gives us His Son to be our life, and we only need to be 'in Christ' for all that is Christ's to become ours. There is only one 'Christian life'—and that is **the life of Christ.** I am never asked to imitate that **Life**, but only to allow Christ to live out His life in me. **'I live, yet not I, but Christ lives in me."**
(Gal.2:20)

(Watchman Nee....The Normal Christian Life)

PEACE

What is peace and how do I get it?

The peace that the world offers requires favorable circumstances and the admiration and approval of everyone you know. This peace is sought and promised but is impossible. The presence of selfishness guarantees the absence of peace. As long as man is focused on survival he cannot find peace even within himself...he cannot truly live.

True peace is impossible without the Prince of Peace, Jesus. The kingdom of God is the place where Peace can be found. When we accept the life of Christ as our own we accept His peace. It is evidenced by the fruit of the Spirit as His nature of love is manifested through His Sons. By faith we are reconciled to The Father through the death and resurrection of Christ and we not only have peace but we bring peace to others. Without a relationship with Almighty God through faith in Jesus Christ there can be no peace.

"Peace I leave with you, My peace I give to you; not as the world gives do I give to you. Let not your heart be troubled neither let it be afraid." (Jn.14:27)

ACTIONS...

I believe you will agree with me that progress is never passive. You may also agree that the majority, if not all, of our actions are essentially reactions to situations, circumstances and personalities that confront us. Our actions are determined by our reactions. Our reactions can be defined as either emotional, logical, or divine.

Our **emotional reactions** are rooted in selfishness. When we operate according to our flesh we make decisions based on what we think is best for us without consideration of the other. When we do make decisions that affect others they are based on what we think is best for them. Since the truth cannot be compromised our emotional reactions result in actions that are made without consideration of godly wisdom and discernment.

Our **logical reactions** are rooted in the intellect of the soul and are usually in opposition to emotional reactions. Compromise is so foreign to the confrontation between the two that the resulting external conflict is evidence of an internal confusion we all experience (Romans 7). As long as we function according to our human nature our actions will be the result of reactions that are evidence of our perpetual dysfunction.

The discernment needed to exhibit the humbleness and humility needed for divine fellowship and unity can be attained only through a relationship with Almighty God through Jesus. The divine perspective on every issue of life is available only to and through the sons of God via divine revelation. The life of Christ is manifested through those who are being transformed into His likeness moment by moment. Our moment by moment decisions become evidence of the power and presence of the Spirit in us as the life of Christ is manifested through us. As overcomers we can sacrifice human emotion and logic for the divine guidance of the Holy Spirit as we engage in "being Christ" to others. Our reactions and decisions result in actions that look exactly like what Jesus would do. We see others with His eyes instead of our own. We believe the gospel not only for ourselves but for those who are still in darkness. This is the ministry of reconciliation. ***"From now on, therefore, we regard no one according to the flesh. Even though we once regarded Christ according to the flesh, we regard Him thus no longer." (2 Co. 5:16)***

LEARNING TO TYPE

When I was 14 yrs. old my mother brought home a used Royal manual typewriter and the textbook that gave instructions for learning to type. I spent the summer teaching myself to type and by the time school began I was typing forty-two words per minute. It took some discipline and was a slow process. I had to first focus on the book and then on the typewriter as I attempted to search the keys and type the practice exercise before I forgot it. At some point my hands and fingers were programmed to hit the right keys without me looking at the typewriter. I found myself able to focus on the book while my hands automatically typed what I saw. I have never forgotten how to type and it now comes naturally at around 55 words per minute.

When I became a "new creation" I had to learn how to ignore my thoughts and tune in to the guidance and direction of the Holy Spirit. I had to focus on The Book and the scriptures therein as I learned to apply the Word to all of the situations and circumstances of life. Over the years I have learned to respond automatically to the Spirit as I remain focused on God's Word. Like learning how to type my hands and feet and entire being is being transformed into the person that God created me to be. I don't make the same mistakes or have the same doubts and fears I used to have. My provision and protection are the responsibility of my Father and He has proven to be everything I need. I am His instrument and He is doing the typing.

If you have been typing since you were 14 it aught to come naturally with almost no mistakes. If you have been saved for years your character and nature should be a reflection of Christ.

"Do not be conformed to this world, but be transformed by the renewal of your mind, that by testing you may discern what is the will of God, what is good and acceptable and perfect." (Rom.12:2)

UNBELIEF

"Jesus answered, 'This is the work of God: that you believe in the One whom He has sent." (Jn. 6:29)

Unbelief is probably the greatest sin when we look at the church. The syncretism that exist in the world today is not foreign to the church. All of the strife and division that exist in the church today is rooted in unbelief. We proclaim our love for The Father and announce that Jesus is Lord of our lives but our actions are not indicative of complete faith and trust in Him and His Word. We volunteer our opinions and post on sports, politics, personalities, events, and circumstances and criticize and blame others in the same fashion that the world does. When the world sees us it is almost like looking into a mirror except that the reflection may be carrying a bible.

Jesus said, 'if you love Me, do what I ask.' Nobody wants to hear a sermon from someone who is not practicing what they preach. If we claim to be ambassadors for Christ we ought to sound like Him and not like everybody else. Our character should be a reflection of the character of Christ. If we believe that God is who He says He is we must also believe that we are who He says we are. Many who will read this and say 'amen' don't really believe but are only agreeing by mental assent. As Paul prayed for the saints at Colosse I pray that the sons of God *'may be filled with the knowledge of His will in ALL wisdom and spiritual understanding; that you may walk worthy of the Lord, fully pleasing Him, being fruitful in every good work and invreasing in the knowledge of God; strengthened with all might, according to His glorious power, for all patience and longsuffering with joy, giving thanks to the*

Father who has qualified us to be partakers of the inheritance of the saints in the light. He has delivered us from the power of darkness and conveyed us into the kingdom of the Son of His love, in whom we have redemption through His blood, the forgiveness of sins." (Col.1:9-14)

According to my bible things will get even worse than they are now. However, I read the end of the story and "in Christ" WE WIN. REJOICE! GOD BELIEVES IN YOU. DO YOU BELIEVE IN HIM? In word and deed....REJOICE.

WHO'S IN CONTROL?

And we know that for those who love God **ALL things work** together for **good**, for those who are called according to his purpose. (Rom.8:28)

Who controls your life? If you answered you do, how is that working for you? Most Christians are familiar with this verse and have committed it to memory. . But do we believe it? Most of us still believe we are in control of our own lives even when we proclaim that 'Jesus is the head of my life." When situations and circumstances don't turn out the way we expected we focus on all the could have, would have, and should haves, analyze the process from a natural perspective and then either beat ourselves up or blame others for the less than perfect results. Our emotional reaction to our misconception of God's divine plan for our spiritual growth leaves us confused and ineffective. Because we fail to view our 'new life' as children of God from an eternal perspective we also fail to realize that when we truly trust God ALL things work out for our good.

God loves you. The question is, do you love Him. The proof of that confession is that we no longer attempt to control our own lives but we allow the life of Christ to manifest itself through us. We can experience the joy and peace of letting go of our desire to know everything and control everything because we trust Him to use the circumstances of our lives to mold us into mature sons of God for the benefit of His plan and purpose. We learn to glorify Him by becoming a blessing to others via a Spirit led life. We KNOW that no matter how a situation looks it is part of God's plan for our good. This spiritual education is only available to those who love The Father more than they love themselves.

Are you a son of the Living God and called to His purpose or are you still trying to control your own life while asking Him to bless the decisions and plans you have made for yourself? Is it all about you or is it all about The Christ in you?

WHO TOLD YOU THAT YOU WERE NAKED?

We are spiritual beings who have a soul and live in a body. Man is made in the image of God and is therefore a spirit. Both our security and significance hinge on our acceptance of God's truth about who He is and who we are because of Him. With our physical eyes wide open we are spiritually blind because the natural man's vision is limited by the closest wall, floor or ceiling. Those physical barriers are part of a world that cannot provide an eternal perspective and leaves us both hopeless and useless as it pertains to God's ordained purpose for His children.

After Adam and Eve disobeyed God they hid from Him. Their reason was that they were naked and afraid. God asked, "who told you that you were naked?" Before Adam sinned he had a different perspective. He saw himself as a spirit with a body (covering) and the concept of nakedness was foreign to him. As an eternal being in time Adam accepted and believed a satanic conversation that was designed to manipulate him into rejecting his Father and living the life of an orphan. He rejected the gospel of the Kingdom for the gospel according to Ray Charles and had to learn to navigate the world blind and with his eyes wide open but without the benefit of the Word. He saw himself as a natural man and not a spirit made in God's image. He believed that he was naked and unprotected and insignificant. He looked to the world provided by Satan to supply those things which he had given up…those things that only The Father could provide.

May I suggest a quick examination of Colossians 1-3. You will discover a description of the children of God who have, by faith, received and submitted to the truth of the gospel of the Kingdom. We are no longer orphans and slaves to the kingdom of darkness but now live in the kingdom of light. We no longer are manipulated by the lies of Satan and the promises of this doomed world but are blessed with an eternal perspective on every situation and circumstance that allows us to manifest the character of Christ as we represent Him in the world. If you don't know Jesus you are naked and you should be afraid. Those who have received Him as their Lord and Savior have "put on" Christ and are covered by His righteousness. Who are you?

"Therefore, as the elect of God, holy and beloved, put on tender mercies, kindness, humility, meekness, long-suffering; bearing with one another and forgiving one another, if anyone has a complaint against another; even as Christ forgave you, so you also must do. But above all things put on love which is the bond of perfection. And let the peace of God rule in your hearts to which also you were called in one body; and be thankful....And whatever you do in word or deed, do all in the name of the Lord Jesus, giving thanks to God the Father through Him." (Col. 3:1-17)

PAY ATTENTION!

*"Do not conform to this world, but **be transformed by the renewal of your mind**, that **by testing** you may **discern** what is **the will of God**, what is good and acceptable and perfect."* (Rom.12:2)

As new creations "in Christ" we have the 'free will' to choose to allow the life of Christ to be manifested through us or function exclusively according to our senses and feelings. Those who live exclusively in the flesh function only as consumers and lack the discernment furnished by the Spirit of God. In that state our senses and consciousness are controlled by our external environment. We either participate in or initiate voluntary drama by playing roles, living out narratives, and reading scripts written by others for us. A universal marketing program tells us what to desire and what to hate. The need to be loved and approved by others dominates our everyday lives. We consciously and unconsciously focus on placing the right thoughts of ourselves into the minds of others. Our Facebook account becomes a testament to our personality. The majority of our actions are driven by what we imagine others may think of us. The unreal image we want others to see in us dictates the way we live. The insanity of this process is verified by the fact that in our dysfunction we struggle to please those who are just as dysfunctional as we are.

As new creations "in Christ" our goal is not to strive to be what others think we should be. Once 'born again' we have no past, our present is empowered and guided by the Holy Spirit, and our future is secure. We are free to be ourselves and that individual credits his/her security and significance to their relationship with Christ. As ambassadors of Christ everything that is true about Jesus is true about us. We don't have to please anyone but our Father. The life of Christ is manifested through the sons of God as they submit to the process of transformation uniquely designed by The Father for each of His sons.

HOW TO GET AN 'A'

The average classroom may be composed of twenty or more students. Not all of those who attend the class are 'A' students. What determines their grade is their performance on any given test. They are then judged by the grade that they received. Since all the students receive the same information and instruction the 'A' students are assumed to be smarter than their counterparts.

Not so in the kingdom of God. According to scripture every 'born again' creature receives a new life. This means a new heart, mind, and spirit. Once a sinner repents of his old life and accepts the life of Christ for himself, he/she becomes a new person with no past, a guaranteed future, and a constant NOW that is guided and directed by the presence of the Spirit of Christ indwelling. Through death and resurrection Christ received an 'A'. Every new born son of God, because he is in Christ and Christ is in him, receives the 'A' that was given to Christ. Because Christ did for us what we could not do for ourselves our performance has nothing to do with the 'A' that we receive.

Once born again, 'in the Spirit' we are all 'A' students and in the Spirit everything that is true of Jesus is true of us.

"Therefore, if anyone is in Christ, he is a new creation. The old has passed away; behold, the new has come. All this is from God, who through Christ reconciled us to Himself and gave us the ministry of reconciliation;" (2 Co.5:17-18)

CONTINUING EDUCATION

It is true of almost all licensed trades that those who hold a license participate in some form of continuing education before that license can be renewed. The purpose of this mandatory training is to protect the public from tradesmen who may be ignorant of new rules, regulations, and procedures that may either prohibit previous practices or enhance professional procedures for the benefit of both the professional and the client. The mandatory continuing education makes the licensed practitioner better at his/her job. The penalty for neglecting this requirement may be a forfeiture of the license to practice.

The church has no such requirement for either leadership or members. Most denominations assume that if a church leader has completed the educational requirements that justify appointment to a certain office or position they are good to go for life. I am not aware of the infilling of the Holy Spirit as one of the requirements for the position of pastor or church leader.

The continuing education of any child of God is possible only via the Holy Spirit. The continuing spiritual growth afforded by the transformation process is in direct proportion to our individual hunger and thirst for the truth. If there is no spiritual growth there is no real growth. Any decision made without the benefit of divine guidance is an exercise in dysfunction.

God purpose for mankind is to glorify Him via sonship. In order for that to happen one needs to GROW UP.

"For though by this time you ought to be teachers, you need someone to teach you again the basic principles of the oracles of God. You need milk, not solid food, for everyone who lives on milk is unskilled in the word of righteousness, since he is a child. But solid food is for the mature, for those who

have their powers of discernment trained by constant practice to distinguish good from evil."(Heb.5:12-14)

AND THE WORD BECAME FLESH (JN.1:1-5,14)

"In the beginning was the Word, and the Word was with God, and the Word was God. He was in the beginning with God. All things were made through Him, and without Him was not anything made that was made. In Him was life, and the life was the light of men. The light shines in the darkness, and the darkness has not overcome it."

The process of transformation involves a change that can be understood as the Word becoming flesh. As we accept the truth and more and more of the kingdom is revealed to us, our soul becomes progressively submissive to our spirit and the nature of our Father is manifested through our flesh by our actions and conversation.

An incomplete existence CANNOT experience the abundant life. Unless one has entered the kingdom of God, His wisdom and discernment is unavailable for clarity in the issues of life. I pray for those who claim to be leaders in the Body of Christ who have yet to realize that:

- Spiritual growth comes to an end in two ways...physical death, or the refusal to grow up in Christ after receiving His Truth. A carnal (immature) child of God is incapable of serving others in his true purpose.
- The church (Body of Christ) is not a building but a spiritual entity that exist to manifest the presence of Christ in a dark world. It is ONE body with no denominations.
- No one individual is endowed with all of God's gifts. Through fellowship and the power and guidance of the Holy Spirit we are used to facilitate the growth of

every child of God. When you think you know everything your ministry is over.

- No matter what your status in life, every man is a slave to either Satan or Almighty God. One lives a life of lies and manipulation that ends in death. The other lives as a slave who is free to be an instrument of the eternal plan and purpose of his Father.
- When we fail to recognize and accept the council of the Holy Spirit our solutions for the issues of this life are incomplete and therefore useless.

My prayer for you and me is that we would become one in Christ as the Word becomes flesh in us.

GROW UP!...SPIRITUAL ADMINISTRATION (Eph.1:3-14)

"All praise to God, the Father of our Lord Jesus Christ, who **has blessed us with every spiritual blessing** in the heavenly realms **because we are united with Christ**. Even before He made the world, God loved us and chose us in Christ to be holy and without fault in His eyes. ***God decided in advance to adopt us into His own family by bringing us to Himself through Jesus Christ***." (Eph.1:3-5)

As 'new creations' we are born into the family of God and by the power of the Holy Spirit, baptized into and made members of the 'body of Christ.' Our old nature is declared dead and buried and we now live as eternal spiritual beings clothed in flesh in time. Because of our union with Christ our quickened spirits are informed by the Holy Spirit and we have the advantage of hearing God and seeing with His eyes. Through the process of transformation our souls progressively submit to the direction and guidance of the Spirit and we look more and more like Christ and His nature is manifested through us.

This is not a smooth transition because of our stubborn desire to manage the process from an intellectual an emotional perspective. We insist on either helping God with the process or impressing Him with our own skillful administration. Our individuality and independence become a hindrance to the manifestation of the personality and presence of Christ through us. When we realize that the world needs to see Him and not us we begin to grow up. The effective administration of true LIFE begins with the acceptance of the Truth of the gospel of the kingdom and the presence of the indwelling Spirit of God.

THE TRUE GIFT

"He came as a witness, to bear witness about the light, that all might believe through Him." (John 1:7)

Creation was designed to host the manifested presence of God in heaven and on earth. The sons of God will always be challenged to walk in the light as He is in the light (1 Jn.1:7). Our trials continually confirm our commitment to walk in and through them...to walk in the light. Compromise is not an option as we walk worthy of the calling to which we were called.

The birth of Jesus was God's greatest gift to men. The world will remain in darkness (ignorance of the presence of God), until the sons of God become the instruments of His plan and purpose and manifest His nature (grace, truth, love) in a way that reveals His light. **Until the "church" learns to live as if EVERYDAY is Christmas, the world will not see Christ through us.**

PERSPECTIVE

"Therefore, from now on, we regard no one according to the flesh. Even though we have known Christ according to the flesh, yet now we know Him thus no longer." (2 Cor. 5:16)

This is the challenge all Christians face daily. We are spiritual beings that still operate in the flesh. We see others with our natural eyes and judge our situations and circumstances according to our feelings. What we have heard about others influences what we think about them. We fail to see them as God does and as a result we cannot help them to discover the truth about their identity. Instead of functioning as a royal priesthood and a holy nation we still look like ordinary men.

"Therefore, if anyone is in Christ, he is a new creation; old things have passed away; behold, all things have become new." (2 Cor.5:17) Our new perspective begins with knowing who we are "in Christ." As sons of God we are available for His use to conform to His plan and purpose for our lives. He is glorified by our obedience as we become Christ to others. As ambassadors of Christ we must learn to look past what we see with our eyes and focus on what God is showing us.

THE PERFECTION OF IMPERFECTION

Our dysfunction as human beings is defined not by the things we see but by the things we do not see. Our failure to understand the trinity of man leaves us incomplete in all our efforts to attain perfection. Man's self-righteousness defines his quest for a perfection that is impossible to attain in the flesh. The truth is only visible through the eyes of God. We seek perfection without knowing what it looks like.

The righteousness (perfection) that we strive for is not available in this world. It is impossible for one who was born in sin and darkness (ignorance of the revealed presence of God), to engage in anything other than the perfection of imperfection. The gospel of the kingdom is the only hope for the walking dead. *"I am not ashamed of the gospel because it is the power of God for the salvation of everyone who believes, first for the Jews, then for the Gentiles. For in the gospel a righteousness from God is revealed, a righteousness that is by faith, from first to last, just as it is written. The righteous shall live by faith."* Rom.1:16-17

Perfection (righteousness) is found only through union with Christ.

NOW!

In the natural we function according to our flesh and as a result we are so preoccupied with survival that we miss the life God intended for us. Our personal quest for provision and protection results in a selfishness that places our welfare above that of all others. The lack of a spiritual relationship with The Father makes it impossible for us to value others above things. In our everyday transactions whatever it is that we can walk away with is more important than the relationship itself. This is not **the culture of the kingdom of God** that should be manifestly evident in the lives of the children of God.

Our present is confounded by our refusal to let go of our past to the degree that we remain uncertain of our future. How long will we remain children who refuse to grow up in the grace our Father offers us? As new creations "in Christ" we have no past and our future is secure. This means that as the Spirit leads us we always live in the 'Now'. As we are transformed into the likeness of Christ we learn to live because survival is not an issue for one in possession of eternal life.

"For I consider that the sufferings of this present time are not worth comparing with the glory that is to be revealed to us. For the creation waits with eager longing for the revealing of the sons of God." (Rom.8:18-19) The grace that we enjoy is the reality of "Christ in us, the hope of glory." The transformation process is designed to result in **a royal priesthood** and **a holy nation**. The

world will see Him through His sons. _Who He is is presently restrained by who He is in._ **GROW UP!**

IGNORANCE: THE COMMON STATE OF MAN

"This is the message which we have heard from Him and declare to you, that God is light and in Him is no darkness at all." (1 John 1:5)

When God proclaimed, "Let there be light" at the inception of His creation it was not to announce the creation of the sun, which was not created until the fourth day, but a proclamation of the availability of the awareness of His presence. The darkness (ignorance of who He is) was not eliminated but exposed by the Truth of the knowledge of the Father who is light. That light is the salvation of men who accept the Truth of God's Word. **Our choice** is to either accept the light or remain in darkness. That darkness promotes a progressive ignorance sustained by the lies that support it.

IGNORANCE (darkness) is one of the root causes of all of life's drama and confusion. Since we all have free will we cannot blame God for our dysfunction if the light has always been available. All of my bad choices and decisions have been the fruit of my own ignorance and fall into three categories:

- IGNORANCE of the truth – I did not know what to do in the situation.
- IGNORANCE of the method of application of the truth – I knew the truth but did not know how to do it.
- IGNORANCE – I knew the truth but did not do it.

"If we say that we have fellowship with Him, and walk in darkness, we lie and do not practice the truth. But if we walk in the light, we have fellowship with one another, and the blood of Jesus Christ His Son cleanses us from all sin" (1 Jn. 1:6-8)

You were created for the purpose of God, The Father, revealing Himself through you. We glorify our Father as we reflect that light and by the power of the Holy Spirit manifest His nature in a world of darkness. The darkness (ignorance) that persist can only be dispelled by the light that shines through the sons of God.

HOW BRIGHT IS YOUR LIGHT?

ONE LIFE

Because we all seek happiness and satisfaction based on our personal understanding of what life should be, even when we achieve the goals we set for ourselves the results are only temporary. The writer of Ecclesiastes summarizes life as meaningless. Many will agree. Our failure to understand the original intent of The Father for mankind results in a selfishness that defines life as meaningless.

When we receive the Truth and believe what the Word says about who we are "in Christ" we are transformed into mature sons of God who fulfill His purpose. We become Christ to others. Through union with Christ our personal needs are met and we are free to love one another as He loved us. Life in and through Christ is the only life that matters and any other existence that is called life is meaningless. THERE IS ONLY LIFE...CHRIST.

"Let us hear the conclusion of the whole matter: Fear God and keep His commandments, for this is man's all. For God will bring every work into judgment, including every secret thing, whether good or evil." (Eccl.12:13-14)

MIND YOUR OWN BUSINESS

We fail to consider the fact that God is a Spirit and because we are made in His image we are also spirits. The spiritual world is more real than the physical world but because we live and think as mere men (in the flesh) we cannot see the kingdom of God. The things of the world that God intended to use to make us aware of who He is and who we are have become objects of praise and worship. Our desires have replaced His desires for us. We have not only forgotten God, we have taken His place. Instead of growing into mature sons of God we mostly remain either ignorant or carnal while criticizing and complaining about things that we cannot comprehend. Instead of loving each other we spend most of our time involved in other folk's business. Our unsolicited opinions and suggestions are catalyst for further contention and division.

When you are blessed with the discernment to look down in front of you and recognize bovine excrement, you have no earthly reason to step in it. As a new creation "in Christ" my existence in this world is evidence of the kingdom of heaven via the life of Christ manifested through me. I have no reason to involve myself in the actions or conversations of those who fail to see the irrelevant pragma of this world as a distraction because for them it is the attraction. His life is now my life. I can be Christ to others because I am in Him and He is in me.

"But we urge you, brethren, that you increase more and more; that you also aspire to lead a quiet life, to mind your own business, and to work with your own hands, as we commanded you, that you may walk properly toward those who are outside, and that you may lack nothing." (1 Thes.4:10-12)

ONLY ONE KIND OF WISDOM

The wisdom of man is like the light of a flashlight. It's brightness continues to fade because the source of the light is a dying battery. God's wisdom brings not only light but life. His light brings first an awareness of your blindness and then an illumination of your circumstances and who you are in them that results in a clarity that is impossible except through divine revelation. The wisdom of God is available to and manifested through the sons of God via progressive revelation.

There is only ONE true wisdom…God's wisdom.

*"For the message of the cross is foolishness to those who are perishing, but to us who are being saved it is the power of God. 'For it is written: I will destroy the wisdom of the wise, and bring to nothing the understanding of the prudent."(*1 Co.1:18-19)

CONTACT INFO: Elder Alex Bess…Dominion Ministries Inc…PO Box 1444, WPB, Fl. 33401… dominionpreacher@gmail.com

91663789R00096

Made in the USA
Columbia, SC
19 March 2018